WHAT TO DO WHEN LIFE KICKS YOU IN THE FACE

By Brian Alexander

Acknowledgements

A special thank you to life... The greatest teacher of all.

Table of Contents

Introduction

Have you ever had one of those days where nothing goes right? How about one of those weeks or years? Or worse yet, an entire life where it seems like everything I do ends in disappointment, chaos and failure. Why me? Who did I cosmically piss off to deserve any of this? These two questions seem to permeate and envelope us as we merely walk or even begrudgingly trudge through the life that has been set before us. Are there ominous forces at work in the world that shape who we are and what we will become, or is it all just chance? Do we all just float around on a breeze or is there someone watching and maybe even planning our every step? Or to take a hint from Forest Gump, is it a little of both? Why do I always seem to get kicked around in life and my neighbor seems to get everything he wants?

As we struggle through our existence the happy, bubbly people around us seem to poke their pointy little noses into our personal space in what appears to be an overly desperate attempt to cheer us up. You know the ones. Everything is always wonderful and they have no clue about the all the hurt that is happening in your life. They say things like "Keep your chin up" or "Your luck will change." Or perhaps its "Look on the bright side" or the proverbial "Its ok, God's in control." Most days we just want them to get smacked in the face with a harsh dose of the reality with which we have been hit, and from which they seem to be so immune.

So why me? Why was I chosen for this hurt or tragedy? Why was I singled out? Is my life ever going to get better? What is the purpose for all of the hurt that exists in the world? These are the questions that steal our peace and keep us up into the wee hours of the morning as we search to find some sort of sense of it all. Throughout our lives the things that hurt begin to compound and grow together to form the framework of how we think and live. Through our younger years each of us builds a set of core beliefs that governs how we will function in life. The events that happen and the things we are taught will frame our reality of the world in which we live. In our adult years we generally follow very closely to the core beliefs that we learned, whether good or bad, from any parental figures or mentors that we had or we will draw from what we learned in church or school. But these core beliefs become challenged as we grow older and sooner or later, life will come along and take what seems to be an ordinary life on a day that seems unlike no other, and kick you – right in the face. These profound moments are the events that shape our destiny and determine who we become. They will determine what we can or cannot accomplish, and ultimately, shape the course of our lives.

Many people are wondering why they can't live what they would consider a normal life. Why everything that they do ends in sadness, pain and regret. Why nothing ever seems to go right for them. I welcome you to our journey. A voyage that takes us into the mind of a life whose core beliefs are being shaped right in front of our eyes. This is my story. This is my search for peace and happiness somewhere on the other side of surrender.

Foreword

This book contains two different stories. These stories are so intertwined with one another that I find it difficult to tell them to you separately so I will alternate back and forth from chapter to chapter with each story until they finally meet up towards the end. The two stories will be labeled Redemption and Revelation.

As you read you will notice that I introduce our spirituality into the story as one of the possibilities on the path towards peace. No matter what your story is, many of us are left wondering why so many people are in pain and why it is either allowed by God or if He caused it. I know firsthand that this can cause an overwhelming feeling of anger, bitterness and disbelief towards God, a higher power, the universe or whatever you wish to call it. This story is written to help you find a balance between religion and your own internal spirituality. It is written to introduce a way of thinking the can bring us through the chaos of life and find that perfect place of peace and balance within the universe.

If you are not a religious person or if you've had a bad experience with God, I would like to ask you to be open to the idea that spirituality could be one of the elements in the answer to your problem. Not that it is, but that it could be. After all, the problems that we have in life were created under our current way of thinking. In order to fix a problem, new ways of thinking must be introduced. Without new concepts or ideas entering our mind, we will stay stuck spinning our wheels as we deal with the same hurts over and over again. A problem cannot be fixed with the same thinking under which it was created.

When you hear the references to God I would like for you to stick with me. No matter how much your mind tries to tell you to put this book down, I need you to push through it. No matter how much you feel your anger towards God and life rise up, push past it and keep going forward because the answers you are looking for are in this book. Keep your mind open to the possibility that something that you may not yet know about life may exist and that you want to know what that one thing might be. As you will see, I too started my journey in that same pain, hurt, sadness, confusion and anger. I hated God and Christians with a passion. My hatred was so great that I may as well have been on the road to Damascus just like the Apostle Paul with papers in my hand to kill any Christian I came in contact with. My desire to find peace and a new way of living is what led me to go deeper than I ever thought I could go. You have that same capacity within you even if you don't know it yet.

The chapters under the label of Redemption will chronicle the story of my life and the redemption of what seemed broken and beyond repair. For many years I used my story as an excuse for why I did not have the ability to change my life. This story will show you that a new life is possible and redemption is available no matter what your circumstances or stories are. I do not tell you my story for shock value or sympathy. My story is told so that you can see how each event in my life created how I functioned as an adult and even dictated the outcome in every situation. As you read each event I would like for you to not focus on the event but see what I came to believe about myself and how those beliefs controlled the future. Some of the stories are sad and some are filled with exquisite joy and beauty. I can't wait to tell you some of those!

The chapters under the label of Revelation will share the

enlightenment that was revealed to me through the process of learning to find peace and healing amidst the troubles in life that seem to follow us and define us. How can I learn to deal with the pain and loss that exist in the world? The sickness or loss of a child... The loss of a house and a home... The loss of a spouse or close relationship... The physical, mental, emotional or spiritual abuse at the hands of another... These all have the capacity to weigh heavily on our minds and affect our well-being for many years to come if not for the rest of our lives.

The process you will read about in these pages has the ability, if applied, to bring you past whatever hardship you have experienced or are experiencing and lead you down the path of perfect peace. I wish you well on this journey and I begin by giving you the phrase that gave me the strength to move forward day after day as I learned to live again. I believe in you! If no one else does and because you may not yet have the capacity to do so for yourself...I do! I believe in you and your ability to go somewhere you have never gone before.

Chapter 1
Redemption

It's Cold Out Here... But it Feels Good

It is a cold winter day. The month is January. It is early 1980's and the air is thick with the talk of the Cold War and the possible spread of Communism. Interest rates are at an all-time high and fear seems to be the predominant emotion being spread across the country. It's only been a few weeks since Christmas. Just enough time for the reality of normalcy to set in and everyone to realize the rush and hype of the holidays are over.

I was a fun loving, somewhat mischievous 10 year old boy living in a large farm house in Eastern Michigan. I always loved to tell people that I lived in the thumb of Michigan due to the fact that Michigan is shaped like a gloved hand.

I was born with blond curly hair which straightened out and turned to a sandy brown by age 4. My eyes were the most interesting shade of hazel and though narrow, usually seemed wide with excitement and wonder. They were squinted as if inquisitively looking deep into a puzzle for a perfectly matching piece or partially closed as if looking into the sun. Eyes like a predator but always searching for something exciting to do or some sort of mischief in which I could dive into head first. Everything I was you could see in my eyes.

I was kind but not gentle; the proverbial rough and tumble boy looking for the next tree to climb, hay loft to swing in, and friends to wrestle and play with. I didn't have many friends and I mostly kept to myself. I never knew why I had so much trouble making connections with other kids. I just thought it was normal. But I was desperately looking for something... something that had eluded me my whole life. Something that I really had no idea I was even looking for. I just knew something was missing.

I grew up in an isolated farmhouse surrounded by over 1,000 acres of fields to freely roam and cause plenty of trouble in. The farmer who owned the land was a gruff but kind elderly man who made his living with corn, soybeans and beef cattle. He rented the old farm house to my family for a modest rate due to the age of the home. The home was over 100 years old and came with its own deep, dark dungeon, an upper attic floor that would scare most people half to death, and all of the creaking and moaning you would expect from a house of that age.

Christmas was not a good time in this home. The stress level always seemed to be maxed out. Maybe due to the fact that there wasn't enough money to afford to buy the presents that were asked for. I'm not sure why, but I guess it was always like that. Maybe it just seemed worse at a time that you thought should be joyous and filled with pleasure. Not in this house. In this house you had to watch your back. You never knew when one of them would snap and the hammer would fall. The hammer seemed to be falling constantly.

And that's when I ended up at a crossroads. There seemed no other choice. All hope was lost. It didn't matter what I did, how hard I tried, or how much I tried to do right... I was going to be beaten. Of course they called it spanking and it was for my own good. I was a bad boy and my attitude had to be reigned in. I had to be broken. My will to rebel must be crushed. I never really understood what that meant when they said it. Like I was a horse or some animal that needed to be brought into submission under their will. And so they tried day after day to break me. To bring me to a point where I would give up my individuality and everything I knew that I was and submit to them. Submit to happily be theirs to do with as they pleased.

So it was as I carried Christmas decorations to the attic that I saw it. As I stared at it, it began to call to me. It was a window – a window out into the unknown – a window that led to something different – a window that could lead to the end of the pain. Wearing nothing but my pajamas I approached the window and stared out at the beautiful, fresh blanket of snow on the ground. The snow shimmered and sparkled as it seemed to call out to me.

The window was old and covered with years of aged layers of paint. I put both hands on the sill and pulled with all my might. The window made a loud crack as it quickly sprung open. I wondered if anyone downstairs heard the loud noise as I stepped slowly out the window and onto the ledge. The snow crunched under the slippers on my feet. The cold air nipped strongly at my face and bare arms. The pain of cold was a numbness that I cherished. The coldness seemed to hide the pain of last nights beating. I walked slowly to the highest point of the tallest peak and looked down to the fresh white powder on the ground below. What would it be like? Could this really end it all? Could it really be over just that quickly?

I sat down on the peak and surveyed the landscape. I had been on this peak before but never when it was this cold or icy. They would kill me if they knew I was up here in such dangerous conditions. The view was incredibly beautiful. A blanket of pristine white, untouched snow covered everything as far as I could see. I stared out across the corn fields at the jagged remains of corn stalks left behind after the harvest, jutting sharply out of the ground like a patchwork fence built by an ancient city trying to defend itself.

The height was impressive. I was so high I could see over

the trees and into the next county. Maybe even into Canada. I looked to the left to see my favorite climbing tree. I had climbed most every tree around but my favorite one had the perfect spot at the perfect height. It had a network of branches that had grown as if specifically ordered as a custom chair for my size. But now, I was even higher than my favorite spot.

And then I looked down – straight down at the ground below. I sat down on the peak and began to ponder what the fallout would be. "Well, if I don't die in the fall, surely they will beat me." My mind raced at what seemed like 100 miles per hour. My mind never really stopped.

I seemed to have the problem of being cursed with the perfect recall of every event that ever happened to me. Other people marveled at my ability to recall everything that I had ever heard and how I was able to remember even the slightest of details as if somehow magic was involved. But not me – to me sleep did not come easy. Night time seemed to be the worst. That seemed to be when the demons came to play. To replay every minute of every episode in the saga that was my life.

As the hair on my arms began to stand up and with the chill of frozen air beginning to take hold on my body, I thought about the first time I remembered being beaten. The first time they tried to break my iron will. The first time they tried to take away my individuality.

Chapter 2
Revelation
The Process of Change

So life is a journey... You and I are on a path... We're on the road of life... We travel the mountain tops and valleys of life... There are so many different phrases out there that try to describe what we're all going through in this thing called life. Patches of happiness scatter themselves in between the 'valleys' of life as we try to make some sort of sense as to why we do what we do every day. I admit that I too wake up sometimes and dread having to brush my teeth and take a shower... again. At this point I have brushed my teeth probably over 20,000 times! What is the purpose of it all?

You have begun to read the story of my life which begins in utter chaos and follows the same boring, monotonous up and down trends day after day. The nagging feeling that there must be something more to life comes and goes but is almost always present in some capacity. It is kind of feeling like you are connected and disconnected at the same time... if that's even possible.

And let's not even start to talk about emotions. Do you ever feel like your emotions dictate everything that you do? Does everyone around you have to know that you are upset or hurt? Whether through passive aggressiveness or not so passive aggressiveness, do you make sure everyone knows what you are feeling? That used to be me. I was a grown man sulking in the corner and pouting because I didn't get my way. But there was a point in time where I learned to take control of my emotions while at the same time being able to completely let go. I know that sounds paradoxical but I am excited about showing you the process that I learned.

To lend some credibility to what I am about to tell you I want to let you know that the man that existed before learning these revelations was an emotionless man whose only friends were indifference, contempt, and a silent rage that could sometimes be not so silent. Anyone who knows me now that did not before would swear to you that there is no way that could be possible. From blinding animalistic road rage to calm natured loving father. This transformation is possible for anyone who is willing to take a closer look at the one place that no one really wants to look – inside. It is human nature for us to look to those around us and ask them to change to accommodate our feelings, wants and supposed needs. But there comes a point that I have to ask myself if I want to try something different. Because as Dr. Phil says, "How's that workin' for ya?"

Looking inside can be a very scary proposition. It is so much easier to look around and place the blame for why we act the way we do on everyone around us. "Well I wouldn't have done this if you wouldn't have done that." "Why would I do that for him if he won't do this or me?" And the cycle continues... for the rest of your life!!! If you had the opportunity to 'get off the ride' so to speak, would you be willing to try something different? What have you got to lose? We spend most of our days shouting at the wind as we tell everyone around us what they need to do to make us happy. And does it even work? No. We will wake up tomorrow, brush our teeth, and do it all over again. Why not try something new?

We all do things on a daily basis that, if we are honest with ourselves, we are not proud of or wish we didn't do. As I look back I remember many mean things that I said to my son as he was growing up. Once those words were uttered I could not take them back. The funny thing about it was that even though I saw the hurt that my words caused my son, I did not apologize for them. I left them there as a wound to fester in his heart. My son was 15 years old the first time I hugged him. That was the day I held him close and told him that I loved him. I had tried to do that many times before but I did not know how to give or receive love. Maybe you also have a strained relationship that you would like to work on? Do you want to wait 15 years to mend a relationship? Have you even considered the hurt that your words cause others or is it all still just about you? Would you rather be right or would you rather be happy? Our desire to win and be right can keep us stuck in destructive patterns for years and even lifetimes. I have an uncle right now that has not spoken with his sister in almost 50 years because of one seemingly minor event. He cannot let go so he cannot experience peace.

Maybe you would like to know how to live your life in a more peaceful manner? Maybe you are that person filled with road rage or are estranged from a friend or family member. Learning the process laid out in this book can bring peace to not only your life but every life surrounding you. So let's dig in by laying the groundwork for everything we will address as we move forward.

This process is going to involve taking a close look inside and before we can do that we need to understand how our mind functions. If I do decide that I would like to have a more peaceful life, how do I replace my current way of thinking for another? I stumbled onto this process after many failed attempts at modifying my behavior to try to be more palatable to those around me. It really is great to realize how much more we are able to learn from failure than we will learn from success. And so, out of my failure, I give you, the process for priming your mind for change.

As we progress it may be easier for you to think about these steps as the mental components needed in life to be able to implement change. Change has the capacity to begin to develop after we prime the engine, so to speak. This set of instructions was born to help others beat the cycles of change that many people seem to be trapped inside. Every time you feel yourself stuck or ready to give up you can take this process and follow the steps to lead you out of the other side of the maze.

Step 1 in the process of any true change has to be an insatiable desire to be a better person. Better for you and better for everyone around you. If you are in a space where you are satisfied with the status quo then there will be no desire to change anything at all. Webster defines insatiable as "To wish, long for or crave". Someone else can't want it for you worse than you want it for yourself. Sort of like a parent with a child that is doing drugs. We may want them to stop more than anything else in the world but we can't make them want it. They have to want it if they are going to show up to rehab, read the books, do the homework and walk the steps to freedom from addiction. Your desire will be your driving force to keep changing even when it is uncomfortable or just plain hurts.

Step 2 – Willingness. Desire usually leads to willingness. I use the word usually because desire can lead to closed minded passion and a justifiable purpose. You know the type. They can say anything they want because they are on a mission from God and they are justified. The problem with knowing everything is that when you do, you can't learn anything. Desire must to lead to a willingness to learn something new. In my experience, this starts by developing a teachable spirit and realizing that we don't have to know all of the answers to everything. Think of it as arguing with a 4 year old. They absolutely know all of the answers and will argue with you adamantly for hours about how dad and grandpa aren't related. It can take some time, but we usually try to teach our children that they don't know everything and that they should be willing to be taught. Unfortunately, most people carry an un-teachable spirit through their teen years and into adulthood. So the questions become, are you willing to learn... or have you not grown up yet? Are you still adamant about your thoughts and beliefs, or will your desire to be a better person lead you to a willingness to learn something new.

There are 3 other areas in which willingness is helpful – The willingness to be wrong, to admit failure and to learn from the failure. Incredible freedom can be found when you open your mind to embrace these 3 moments as they happen. It is ok to not have all the answers. It is ok to let someone know that I screwed up. Failure has the capacity to show me something new about myself and does not mean that I am a failure. I have learned so much through my failures in life that I have come to call them necessary failures. Some failures must happen to bring us to where we need to be in order for our next success to occur.

Step 3 – Openness. The opposite of being open is adamancy. There is no room for adamancy on the path to peace. Webster defines adamancy as "Utterly unyielding in attitude or opinion in spite of all appeals." In this mindset it doesn't matter what information anyone shows you, your mind is unmovable. Vera Nazarian said "If you have never changed your mind about some fundamental tenet of your belief, if you have never questioned the basics, and if you have no wish to do so, than you are likely ignorant."

The problem then becomes that the more convinced we are that we are right, the more we will fight for what we think is right. If you find yourself fighting for what you believe then this may be a belief that you need to step back and take a look at. Craig Groeschel said "Many times we would rather feel that we are great than admit that we don't know and learn something new about ourselves." It can be hard to put a long standing belief to the test but that is what the process of change is all about. Maybe your belief will hold up under testing and maybe it will not. That isn't really the point here. What matters is that you are willing to put your idea on the block to be tested, tried and changed if necessary.

Another good reason to be open is that we only know what we know and we don't know what we don't know. Did anyone follow that? What we don't know, we don't know that we don't know it. And what we don't know about, we do not have the capacity to change or attempt to fix. Without openness we cannot reach awareness. And it just so happens that awareness is step 4.

Step 4 – Awareness. True openness has the ability to activate the receptors in our minds which leads to an awareness that did not previously exist. Have you ever wondered where the saying came from that you can't teach old dogs new tricks? There are just so many statements that fit in here. I'm a leopard and I've found my spot. This is just who I am, take it or leave it. Sometimes it seems easier to just tell people to deal with us rather than to actually take a closer look at the impact that my choices and actions have on those around me.

Have you ever looked around yourself and thought about how many people you know that just aren't very self-aware? I was in a conference once with several thousand people and the speaker asked everyone to raise their hands if they ever felt that they were self-deceived or did not see themselves very clearly. About 5% of the people raised their hands. He then asked people to raise their hands if they knew of someone else who was self-deceived and over 90% of people raised their hands. So 90% of us know someone who is self-deceived but only 5% of us are actually aware of self-deception. It sounds to me like we either have a math problem or a perception problem.

Think about the story of King David from the Bible. This man was so unaware of his effect on other people and so self-involved that he slept with another man's wife, had the husband killed to cover up the fact that she got pregnant, and then married her! It was not until someone came to him and pointed it out that he realized that what he had done was wrong! How crazy is that! He never stopped even once to think that this was wrong! This is just one example of how blind we can be and not even have a clue that we are blind. It is an example of how we can lose our way but think100% for sure in our minds that we know exactly where we are. If I asked you to raise your hand, which group would you be in? All my friends are unaware but I am completely aware? Or is it time to realize that I only know what I currently know! Can you accept the fact that without new knowledge and information added into your mind, you can't improve your position in life or solve any of your problems? What if the only way to move forward is to introduce something new?

So what is the best way to begin to remove my adamancy and open my mind to self-awareness? One way is to allow for the 5-10% chance that I could be wrong in every situation. After all, there may be a critical piece of information that I am missing that will change my opinion. Allowing for this chance that I could be wrong will change my presentation from I am right, to I believe I am right. Based on the information I currently have this is what I believe. Anyone can now add new information and my mind will be open to receive it. Presentation of your ideas will change from adamant to respectful and people will begin to see you as someone they would like to hear from as opposed to the guy who is always beating everyone up with his opinion. Believe me. I've been that guy.

Step 5 – A Trustworthy Friend. Step 5 adds a component that can be difficult for almost anyone. You must find a friend that you can trust to speak the truth about what they see into your life. Because it is so difficult for us to see ourselves clearly and we are often self-deceived, we need someone else to tell us what they see. Now I think you know where I'm going with this. This can't just be anyone who is a 'yes man' and says you look good no matter what. This must be someone that you believe is ahead of you on the road you would like to be on. What do I mean by that? Well, if you have a problem with road rage your mentor should not be in an anger management class. If you would like to be a more positive person than your mentor should not be berating everyone they see as you walk through the mall. If you would like to grow spiritually your mentor should be reading more than people magazine. In other words, choose your mentor wisely.

One way to recognize a friend who can be a great mentor is that they will ask a lot of questions and they will not make too many absolute statements. A great mentor rarely gives advice because then the answer would belong to them which does not offer you mental ownership of the idea or ideal. Questions provoke thought and give you the capacity to create a new reality for yourself. Do not fool yourself into believing that you can do this on your own. When you cannot see yourself in a clear way, a good friend will "clean and adjust the mirror" to help you see yourself more clearly.

Step 6 – Paradigm Change. A paradigm is the model, structure or framework under which all of my thinking occurs. Simply put, if I believe I am a duck, I will act like a duck. If I believe no one loves me and I am a failure, what will I be? That's right – un-loveable and a failure. Once we have removed the adamancy of our previous ways of thinking and allowed for awareness to begin to settle in, we are primed for change in the way we actually see our world. Let me try to give you an example. If I go to work every day believing that the boss is upset with me and that I can't do anything right, will my performance be affected by my perception of the situation? Of course it will. Alternately, if I believe my position is secure, that I am completely capable and I am thankful for a great job, how will my performance be? I hope you can see that my paradigm, how I see my situation, will affect how I act. We're going to dig a lot deeper into this in a later chapter so stay tuned. Two very important areas of change we will look at will be changes in the way I think and changes in the way I act. I can't wait to get there!

Step 7 – Implement changes. Step 7 is really the most important of all steps because without it nothing will ever actually happen. If we never implement any of the changes then this is all just a mental exercise. At some point, what we are learning about ourselves needs to be brought from the proving ground of our minds to the testing grounds of reality. Einstein's definition of insanity is "Doing the same thing over and over expecting a different result." As you have realizations about your life and see changes that need to be put in place, don't wait.

New Year's resolutions have become a detriment to timely change throughout the year. We take items that could be life altering and relegate them to one day a year. Studies show that even this system is flawed as the average New Year's resolution lasts less than 30 days. You may ask, "Well what am I supposed to change Brian?" As we move forward I will be offering new thoughts and ideas that will provoke thought in your life and give you plenty of things to work on to keep you busy. I know this sounds a little unnerving but I promise you that you are going to love it once you get started!

The most important thing to remember about implementing a new change is that from time to time you will fail. Yes that's right. Not everything you try is going to work every time. And that's ok. As I said before, failure should be viewed as nothing more than a building block on the way to success. This can be difficult to process for those of us who had an overbearing parent or if we tend to put extremely high expectations on ourselves. If I start to eat an ice cream cone and I drop it on the ground do I stop instantly and say "I'm never eating ice cream again!" Of course not, that would be ridiculous. The same thing goes for change. Sometimes you will implement some change in your life and you will fail. Don't quit. Failure gives us the opportunity to learn. Sit down with your friend / mentor and let them walk with you through your failure. This will help you determine where you went wrong and choose a new plan to implement for tomorrow. The most important thing though is... Don't Quit! Keep moving through the process. A good exercise to start your mind headed in this direction is to write a few things down about your current state of mind. Go ahead and spend a few minutes to write down 3 things, areas of your life, or relationships that you would like to be better. Next, write down 3 reasons that your mind gives you for not making changes in these areas.

Chapter 3
Redemption

The Child Within – How it All Began

I was born in 1972 in East Chicago, Indiana. I was the second of 4 rough and tumble, knock-down, drag out boys. Dad had just returned from Vietnam and was heavy into drugs and alcohol. It seemed he was looking for anything to cover up the pain inside. He talked very little about what happened over there but was a very angry man with a temper that flared at the slightest of infractions. He took a lot of pride in how he had raised his boys to be so strong with absolutely no hint of weakness or emotion. Women acted weak and emotional, men had to be strong. Men didn't cry – men didn't whine – men did not show affection. Those things were for women only!

Mom had a sickly childhood and developed many different diseases that always had her hopped up on prescription drugs. She was always sick with something. Sometimes up, sometimes down, 'you just never knew what you were gonna get.' She was very confused herself about what love was and how to give it. The worse the relationship got between mom and dad, the more she acted out against us kids. The only thing we boys seemed to get on a regular basis from them was admonition and discipline – lots of discipline. These are two very important building blocks for a child but without adding nurturing and love to the equation, it can cause hurt, anger, and distrust. Affection was not a norm in this house. Hugs were rare, kisses non-existent, and the phrase 'I love you' was only used as a cruel addition to the 'This is going to hurt me more than its going to hurt you' speech usually said jokingly – as if it was funny.

My parents made it very clear through their actions and most of what they taught, that everything was about them and what us boys could do for them. Whoever did the best job of providing for them would rise to the prestigious platform and be crowned with favorite son status. That was until you said or did something to knock you down and then it was back to the bottom.

We were moderately poor growing up and we were taught that the number one goal in life is to "get all you can, can all you get, and sit on the can." "Look out for number one and crush anyone who gets in your way." "Only the strong survive."

The strange thing about growing up in a chaotic home is that you don't know it's not normal. All of the screaming and fighting seem like a normal part of everyday life - until you go over to a friend's house. We lived in chaos completely unaware that there is an alternative to this ungodly pattern of power hungry warlords fighting for position and the ability to one up everyone else in the family.

In the summer of 1975 there was a change in the household. This house found Jesus. Or so they thought. What was actually found was an extension of the chaos that they were already in. The family entered with blind faith into a religion that oppressed the week and rewarded the strong with the position of oppressor. It was a right wing fundamentalist church. This religion reinforced the fact that at the core, every person is evil, and cannot possibly live up to the standards set by God unless we constantly punish and deny ourselves. And so the punishment begins.

Dad and mom joined a Bible college and quickly progressed through the ranks by learning how to manipulate others to do what you wanted them to do in order to further your own agenda. The tools most widely used were guilt, shame and condemnation. In their eyes everything was an absolute. There was no room for gray areas to them, only black and white. There was a specific answer for everything and no room for anything that was outside of that box. Anything outside of that box was strictly forbidden and deemed 'Of the world' and thus was not allowed.

Now we step back into the world that was created for me. There is a long list of things that are forbidden and none of them comes with a sufficient explanation as to why they are forbidden. I was curious and as any child, I yearned to know the answer to the age old question. Why? Why can't I do this? Why can't I do that? My questions went unanswered. Questions to them were a sign of rebellion. "We don't ask questions" I often heard them say. "We just do what we are told."

By age 4 I was enrolled into a "Religious School". It was their sole responsibility to make sure that I was brought up in their ways. To be brain washed into believing what they believed without asking questions. To remove from my mind and soul any desire to think or make decisions on my own. Their basic form of driving home their ideology was a combination of repetition and physical punishment. The worst part about the punishment was that it usually came without any warning or explanation of the wrong that was done. I longed to know 'Why'. Maybe the answer to 'Why' would somehow help me find my place in this chaotic world full of pain and disappointment. This was the soundtrack stuck on play in the deep, dark places of my mind as I pondered the simple question. "Should I freeze to death on this roof – or create a masterpiece of deep red blood on the beautiful white blanket of snow below?"

Your homework for this chapter is for you to go back to the beginning and write down some of the overarching thoughts or ideas such as religion or parental issues that existed in the home you grew up in. I remember the first time I did this exercise and had the amazing realization that much of what I believed was based on false information given to me as a child. As we continue I will share many of those false beliefs with you in an attempt to help you identify your own. But for now, just think back to the framework of your childhood as you look to identify your early influences.

Chapter 4
Revelation

Surrender – What is it and Why?

Whenever we embark on a journey to try to dig a little deeper into our minds in an attempt to find some sort of solid ground to stand on, we eventually run into thoughts about our spirituality. So many times we hear people talk about the hole in our souls that can only be filled by God. We hear them talk about a feeling of being incomplete or kind of a knowing that there is something else out there. Well, I too have experienced that feeling. I have laid awake many nights staring at the ceiling wondering if there was a God. I even remember thinking that if God does exist, He must really hate me. After all, what had I done in life that was really so terrible? I had never killed anyone and I had even tried really hard to do a lot of good to make up for the bad that I did do.

As we ponder these thoughts about spirituality we may even take that next big step and decide to visit a church to find out what it's all about. Maybe you grew up in church and can talk the lingo or you have absolutely no idea what it's all about. It doesn't really matter at this point because we are just going to stick our pinky toe in to see what the water feels like.

As we embark into this very different world we will sadly, in many cases, run face to face into something very different than the spirituality that we are looking for – We run into Religion. Religion has a great capacity to further fracture our soul by introducing more issues into our mind than already existed. For years I tried to walk the path of religion and did not experience any peace. In fact, all I remember experiencing was judgment, guilt and condemnation. But thankfully it wasn't all in vain. I began to focus on a specific word that had been offered to me by religion that turned my focus in a different direction. The word was surrender.

At first glance this word seems like it really doesn't have any application in my life unless I'm deadlocked in a battle with a force that I cannot defeat... that's when it hit me. I am deadlocked in a battle with a force that I cannot defeat. I am deadlocked in a battle with my mind. Every day I fight against it as it tells me what an idiot I am, or how I could have done it just a little bit better, or how I'll never do it good enough. Every day I strive and work hard for success as my mind tells me one of two things. Either I don't deserve it and that I'll never make it or that I do deserve it and I am allowed to be ruthless and crush anyone in my way. Either way, my mind is pitted against me in a battle for what it wants me to believe about myself. Why is my mind so evil and out to get me? Great question. We'll get to that a little later.

Let's get back to surrender. What if I asked you right now "Are you surrendered"? Some of us would emphatically answer "Absolutely" or "Of course I am". I go to church. I read the Bible and pray. Others would ask "What the hell are you talking about. What do I need surrender for? That's only for religious people." But what is surrender? Is it simply doing the things that you think are good? Is it not doing something that you want to do? Surrender is defined by Webster as giving oneself up into the power of another or to yield to the power possession or control of another.

The reality is that each of us may have a different idea of

what surrender is. What many people fail to realize is that our current reality is based on many different factors. The world we live in, the events from our past, and the present circumstances we encounter all shape our ideas of who we think we are. It also shapes how we think the world works and the relevance that big words like surrender will have for us or mean to us. Let me give you an example. Consider a child that was raised by loving, nurturing parents. This child's understanding of love and the way they give love to others will be drastically different than a child that was neglected or abused. Because of this it is important to really take some time to understand what surrender currently means to you and what application it can have in the future.

The truth is that while on the journey for surrender people will get lost and found many times. Surrender is not so much of a destination as it is a way of thinking. A way of thinking that leads to freedom and peace of mind. The mind... did I really have to bring him into the discussion? To many the mind is a cruel host. He brings to light that which we don't want to see. He reminds us of our wrongs and keeps alive the battle that rages from within... the battle for my thoughts and the battle for my soul.

I know this all sounds a little cryptic but I promise you I'm going somewhere. We wonder as we walk through life and experience sadness and pain, "Why can't I be happy?" "Why can't I have peace?" Why does everything bad always happen to me?" Where do these thoughts come from? Do they generate from thin air in an attempt to control me? Are they planted there by an evil scientist or aliens? The answer, of course, is no. Every thought generates from the mind as it produces thoughts and ideas in an attempt to create something out of nothing, control out of chaos, or to meet the perceived needs of its host. The mind is the most powerful thing on the planet. With one idea the steam engine was born and ushered in a new era of production and growth that changed the world. With one thought of superiority in an evil mind a plan was born to exterminate entire races of people and an attempt forged to take over the world. The mind truly is the most powerful implement that exists in the world.

So the next question becomes, if it is my mind that is controlling me, how do I turn the tables and control it? Great question and I'm so glad you asked because I have an answer... an answer that has the ability to lead anyone to peace. That is anyone who wishes to have peace. You might say, "Well of course I want peace Brian, why wouldn't I want peace." Well, if you think about it, many people have trouble functioning well in a peaceful environment. This leads them to constantly need to create drama in their lives. Let's look at an example. We'll take a look at a friend of mine that we will call JT who grew up in a chaotic home. He grew up with yelling, screaming, and chaos of all kinds. Now as an adult, every time things are quiet he feels out of place. He feels like something is wrong. So what does he do? He picks a fight. He starts an argument in the work place. He makes something up about someone else and spreads it around the office. All of this is done in an attempt to create drama and chaos and feel somewhat comfortable. But deep inside JT is hurting. He confides in me that he is emotionally very empty. He wishes that he knew what it felt like to be happy. He wishes he knew what it felt like to be sad. He doesn't know either... just emptiness. He wishes he didn't feel awkward when someone tries to be kind to him or give him a hug.

Author Henri Nouwen introduced the idea that inside most people is a voice screaming out for help over and over and hoping that someone will notice and come to the rescue. Hoping desperately that someone will come hold us tightly and make everything better. But we find incredible solace in the fact that no one can hear us screaming. And so we go through life with a half-hearted smile on our face constantly inventing and re-inventing the persona that we show to the world.

Victory over the mind is not only possible but it is very highly probable. In the beginning I too thought that peace would never be available for me. Maybe you also believe that you've done too much or that too much has been done to you to be able to gain freedom from the things that plague your mind and your life. Along this journey we will walk step by step down the path that leads to peace. I remember early on in my journey being told by a psychiatrist that all I had to do was to take all my problems and leave them at the foot of the cross and give them to Jesus. Great suggestion but he failed to give all of the steps detailing how to make that happen. What am I supposed to do? Give me a box and some duct tape. I'll wrap up all my problems in the box and tape it up very tightly and leave it... now where is that cross at? I know I saw it somewhere. And now all my problems are magically gone. Of course I'm being facetious but my point is that there are so many religious statements that exist that have absolutely no power because they didn't come with the instructions or steps on how to make it work. God is in control. Great... my daughter is having seizures in the hospital... is it his fault? How does that help me or bring me peace? What an arbitrary statement to say to someone in a crisis. What a thoughtless comment to someone in pain that has no clue who God is. The only conclusion a person could make from that statement would be that this is all His fault and 'me and Him are gonna have some words.'

So what does surrender mean to you? You may even be thinking, "What am I supposed to be surrendering?" Do I just wake up one day and say "I surrender" and everything is all better? Not exactly. It actually helps to think of surrender as an ongoing process and not an event. It would be great if there was fairy dust to just sprinkle over our heads and everything was better. But if we view surrender as a destination that can be fully attained, we will stop when we think we have arrived and be filled with pride for having reached the goal. Seeing surrender as a process will help to keep me searching for the true goal of victory over the mind.

When I hear the word surrender I instantly think of two

forces that have been locked in battle for a long time and one of the forces finally reaches the point that they just can't take any more. They are battered, bruised and torn apart so they decide to waive the white flag and resign their campaign. So that leads me to ask another question. Who or what am I supposed to be surrendering to and why? What if things are going pretty good and I am comfortable with how my life is going? Do I really want to mess with my life if things are going ok?

The problem here is that most of us will not head down this path unless there is an event or series of events that forces us to reevaluate our lives. The desire to change does not come out of thin air. It comes out of the hurt, pain or sadness that we are currently experiencing or a culmination of what we have experienced in the past. This is where I will introduce the word that leads to true surrender... brokenness. It may be hard to hear, but some sort of catalyst must be involved to bring us to the point where we decide to make changes. When we feel that everything is going ok there isn't a reason for us to change. Until the pain of remaining the same exceeds the pain of change then we will not choose change.

Most likely if you're reading this book you can identify with the title and the idea of life kicking you in the face. This is the moment that you are already down on your knees and hurting from a series of events that have led you down a path that is the opposite of what you would have considered happiness and success. And then life in its cruel irony doesn't decide to go pick on someone else. It comes closer and rares back with its size 19 combat boots, and kicks you right in the teeth. The pain is overwhelming and really more confusing than anything else. And then we ask questions like "Why me God" and maybe even vent our frustration and anger towards Him and anyone else that may come into our path.

These are the moments that have the potential to define who we are. These moments are the catalyst that can allow us the opportunity to raise the white flag and decide to make changes. I use the word opportunity because you get to choose when you will raise the white flag. My process for brokenness took 5 years because I refused to raise the white flag. With every blow I built more defenses and constructed new offenses to fend off the attack. I didn't know that I needed to surrender. In fact, it never crossed my mind because I thought I was completely in control. I didn't know that there was a battle raging for my mind and my soul. And so I kept on fighting the fight thinking that this is what life is all about and that it wouldn't be over until I finally drew my sword and slew the dragon in dramatic fashion.

So what is your event? What fight is going on in your life that you are close to being ready to give up? Is it the failure of a relationship or the inability to maintain a healthy relationship? Either one can lead you to believe that no one loves you or that you are not a lovable person. Is it the loss of a job, a business or an investment? Are any of these making you believe that you're a failure because of your inability to provide for your family? Maybe you are coming to terms with a painful past or lost childhood and the realization that no one has ever really loved you or showed you how to love others. It doesn't matter what it is. All that matters is that you reach the point where you decide that you would like something different with your life. Then and only then is the stage set for something to take place in your life that is beyond our control. Something absolutely amazing!

Chapter 5
Redemption

The First Time – Insignificant Tears

My mind continued to race on its track stuck in a downward spiral to what I thought could be the end of everything. A little more courage and it could all be over. A little less fear and the pain could be at an end.

I remember the summer of 1976. I had just turned 4 years old. This is usually a wonderful period of growth and wonder in a child's life; a time where they look for answers to their questions about life and living; a time of living and laughing without knowing about all of the harsh realities that await us out in the world. But apparently, that wasn't the path that I was going to walk. For some reason I was chosen to walk a different path. A path that I didn't understand and didn't really know was different from how everyone else lived.

The day is the 4th of July. The excitement of fireworks and a family picnic is brimming over as I waited for all the family to arrive. Everyone is going to be here today – all of the grandparents, a few aunts and uncles, and all of the cousins. The day was nothing but fun as we ate, played and laughed. That is until one of the tattletale cousins, also known as the "religious police", decided that I had done something wrong and that the parents needed to be notified. I really don't even remember what it was that I had done. I only remember that a tribunal was called and I was charged as guilty and sentenced to be punished. Because the infraction took place in front of others, Judge Dad decided that I must be punished in the same manor. I was told to assume the position bent over the chair with hind end sticking out and ready to be swatted.

This is where things start to get confusing. Most young boys are taught that men are tough and don't cry – especially in front of other people. And as the anger of being tried, convicted and punished in public begins to swell and the confusion of not knowing what I had done and why it was wrong mounted, I made a drastic decision. I was not going to give them the satisfaction of seeing me cry. This was the essence of me. I was inquisitive and curious and I wanted answers. They had to tell me 'why' or I was going to rebel. This decision proved to be the beginning of a battle that would rage for many years to come – a battle of defiance over independence, individuality, and 'Why'.

As the spanking began I tried to anticipate each swat as I gritted my teeth and tensed every muscle in my body in an attempt to alleviate the pain. Everything seemed to be going well. I was strong and knew I could 'take it like a man.' A few more swats and it would be over. Then came the words that enraged dad and sparked the war – "Look, He's not crying". The words were spoken by grandpa and seemed harmless enough. They lacked meaningful harm as they were spoken but didn't have the effect they were intended to have. Dad turned me around and looked deep into my eyes with a scowl and said "You think you're tough? Well I guess we'll have to break him." "Break Him?" – I thought – like I was a dog needing to be housebroken or a wild stallion being forced to resign myself to captivity and a saddle.

The spanking's intensity increased but I still refused to give in to this embarrassment. And that's when it happened. One of the most feared sounds on the planet was heard by me for the first time. The sound of a belt being unbuckled and pulled quickly through the pants loops. "Fttttttttttttt." My confusion grew as the events unfolded. Why was dad taking off his belt? What was going on? Why was all of this necessary? The belt was then folded in half and applied swiftly and repeatedly to my back side. The pain was unlike anything I had ever felt before. I knew it would not be long. The tears could not possibly hold out against this type of pain.

The belt, as it turns out is a very inaccurate weapon. It doesn't stop where it starts. The end of the belt can continue around the thigh, to the stomach and hips, or wrap around a leg. At the end of the belts travel its stops abruptly with a crack like lightning and a sting that travels down the legs to the feet and half way up the back. Of course the belt is no respecter of appendages as it will grab an unwary arm, hand or finger if it decides to try to protect the areas in danger and in pain.

The lightning crack at the end is what it seemed dad enjoyed. His teeth gritted in anger as he strained to get every ounce of energy into the swing. My teeth gritted in pain as every fiber of who I was tried to avoid the inevitable. And then the tears came. But these were no ordinary or insignificant tears and neither where they the tears of brokenness, sorrow or repentance. These were tears of anger and defiance. These tears had meaning and belief attached to them. These tears told me who I was and in an ironic way did exactly the opposite of what tears were meant to do. These tears did not cleanse and free me to be who I was created to be. These tears were prophetic as they posed a question in my thoughts and deep within my mind. "Am I really that bad of a person? Am I on the same level as any animal that is being beaten into submission? I must be a really bad boy."

Now while many people might focus on the event that just occurred, the more dangerous component is the belief that begins to take root in the mind. If I believe that I am bad then sooner or later that is what I will become. It may even be difficult to remember which one came first. Was I always bad or did I actually become a bad person because it is what I came to believe about myself?

Your homework for this chapter is to get somewhere quiet for a minimum of 30 minutes and write down what you have come to believe about yourself. Write down the words 'I am' and then continue with whatever comes into your mind. It can be positive or negative. It doesn't matter because either can keep us from reaching our full potential. The important thing is to be sure that you are honest with yourself and dig deep. Your defining event may be from this year or it could be from when you were a child. Go as deep as you need to go to find the moments that planted belief into who you are and changed the course of your mind.

Chapter 6
Revelation

Brokenness – The Unknown Plan

As we look around the world and see pain and sadness we often wonder how God could allow such things to occur in the lives of those He says He loves. Why do bad things happen to good people? Why does hurt and pain exist all around the world? If God is in control and He does love us than why doesn't He make everything a utopia full of butterflies and flowers? When we pose these questions to the religious crowd there are several theories and standard answers that instantly come to the surface. There is the belief that the devil is in control of this earth and running around causing trouble and God just can't do anything till he comes back to set everything right. There is also the belief that God is punishing those who just can't seem to be good enough or do enough to please Him. And then there are those that say that God is in control and that He has a plan for everything that happens. This only leaves us wondering what that plan is and why wasn't He there when I needed Him. Where was He when my dad was beating the hell out me? Where was He when you watched your loved one die a slow painful death? Where was His protection when your loved one died in an accident?

Well I would like to take some time to pose my theory and it really is a combination of what was mentioned above with the idea mixed in that we were never really meant to have a definitive answer to the question "Why God". We can start down this path by looking at the story of Job from the Bible. I have always struggled with the idea that God allowed Satan to have free reign in Job's life just to prove a point and settle a bet.

The story of Job begins with God asking Satan if he had noticed how faithful Job had been to God. Satan quickly retorts that if Job didn't have all of the wealth that God had provided him that he would not be so faithful. God quickly comes back with the challenge of "I'll bet he would". And so God removed his hand of protection from Job and allowed Satan to take away everything that Job had even though Job had done nothing wrong and was the pride and joy of God himself.

No matter how many times I batted this around in my head I just couldn't understand why God would make a bet with the life of someone he loves and claims to be so proud of. I originally pondered this question as I read a great book called Disappointment with God by Philip Yancey. A great read if you are stuck in a place where you are angry with God.

So now Job has lost everything. He is sitting in a trash heap covered in sores and looking for any type of relief. And to compound matters his 'friends' show up to tell him that he is being punished by God so he must have done something wrong. How many of us have had that wonderful friend... (biting my tongue). I actually once had a friend that told me that the reason my life was messed up was that I wouldn't listen to him. Wow!!! They then proceed in all their infinite wisdom to tell him exactly what it is that he has done wrong and what he continues to do wrong. That is until God finally shows up... in chapter 38. Chapter 38!!! Are you kidding me? Where have you been God? My life has been ripped to pieces and you wait until chapter 38 to show up. I reached my limit way back in chapter 25 and I needed you to come in with the cavalry back then. Job has been asking "Why me God" for 37 chapters and listening to idiots try to tell him why!

So what does God say when he finally shows up? He first addresses all of the people who gave bad advice to Job by saying "Who is this that obscures my plans with words without knowledge?" This tells us two things. First, God had a plan for what happened with Job. Second, when someone is experiencing pain, don't presume to know the will of God and be like Job's friends. God then continues with what I believe is one of the most impactful and, if we apply it, one of the most freeing passages in scripture. If you're not a fan of God or scripture I still want you to stick with me through this. We actually are going somewhere great! I promise. God spends the next few chapters asking Job if he can explain how the universe works.

Where were you when I laid the earth's foundation?
Who shut up the sea behind doors?
Have you ever given orders to the morning?
Have the gates of death been shown to you?
Do you know the laws of the heavens?
Can you set up God's dominion over the earth?
Who provides food for the raven when its young cry out to God?

God then lets Job know that until he can explain any of this that he cannot give him the answer to "Why me God". He could attempt to tell us but we would not be able to understand. The only thing we can do is trust that he does have a plan somewhere in the midst of what we experience. Even Paul in the New Testament talks about the wonderful mystery of God and the things about God that we were not meant to know. If we knew all of the answers than trust really wouldn't be necessary would it. Perhaps Job was called to a higher purpose. Throughout his ordeal even his wife said that he should curse God and die. Maybe God chose him and asked him to suffer so that his story could be told for thousands of years to come to help show others how big the plan of God really is. His story has the capacity to offer hope to anyone who is hurting. Hope that somehow God has a plan that is bigger than me or what I am going through. That perhaps somewhere at the end of this storm there is a rainbow and maybe even a surprise leprechaun with a pot of gold.

Surrender comes in to play when I decide that I don't have to know what the plan is to be appeased. As long as I am asking God why this is happening to me it is not possible for me to be at peace because I still am looking for the "Why". Many people will agonize for years and even lifetimes over this question. They will become old and bitter and every painful step through life will resound the question... why

So what if Job had not embraced his pain? What if he had tried to run from it or go around it? What if he had listened to his wife and ended his life? What if God has asked you to experience some suffering so that he could teach you something about yourself? What if God has asked you to experience some suffering so that he could teach you something about Himself? Would you be willing to embrace that pain and walk straight through the center of it? Job did. Job embraced his pain and in chapter 38 he ended up with an amazing payoff. He heard the voice of God.

I love the quote from King Arthur in the movie First Knight. "There is a peace that can only be found on the other side of war." I contend that there is a peace that can only be found on the other side of our pain. And like the old children's song goes – You can't go around it. You can't go under or over it. You have to go right through the middle of it and feel every agonizing moment of it if you are to get what it is that God has for you to learn about yourself. Our gut reaction to pain is to avoid it and find anything possible to cover it up. A relationship, alcohol, partying, active social life, withdrawal, drugs, internet, and even serving others in a church can be used to run from the pain.

So if one of God's purposes in the pain that we experience is to implement the plan that he has then the next obvious question is "What is his overall plan for the suffering in my life?" I would like us to change our thinking on this to the broader sense of the question. Why do we all experience conflict on a daily basis? Conflict seems to exist everywhere we go and no matter what we do we can't seem to get away from it. It exists in our homes, in our churches, at the workplace, in our cars on the road, and in practically every relationship that we experience. Couldn't God have made things a little bit easier? Well the truth is that He actually did. He originally created the Garden of Eden which was a perfect utopia where God provided everything, including meeting our four basic needs.

There are four basic needs in life that we search to have met on a daily basis. Every need that exists in life stems out of one of these four as its base desire. The four basic needs are love, acceptance, worth, and security. Every day Adam and Eve went directly to God to get those needs met. Now let's focus for a second and think about how we feel about each of these needs from the second we wake up in the morning till the second we go to bed.

The 4 Basic Needs

- **Love** – Being loved the way we want to be loved
- **Acceptance** – Being accepted the way we want by our peers, parents, and God
- **Worth** – Having a balanced sense of self-worth and believing that I matter
- **Security** – Feeling safe socially, financially, and in our close relationships

You'll notice that the acronym for these words is L A W S. This makes the words easy to remember and also reminds us that when we attempt to get any of these needs met from any relationship other than God then we are placing ourselves and the other person under the law and in conflict. The solution to our problem begins with having a change in thinking. It begins with opening our minds to the possibility that God is the only one that has the ability to meet these four needs. Now you don't yet have to believe this. You even have my permission to jump up and down and scream out loud right now and call me an idiot. But if your mindset and issues in life were created by the way you currently think, what would be the harm in trying something different?

Have you ever been in a relationship where someone was trying to make sure that you were meeting one of these needs for them? The pressure to perform is intense. This is when we feel the weight of being under the law and sooner or later you are going to let that person down and that is when we fall into conflict. Let's dig a little deeper into the story of Adam and Eve and you'll start to see why I say that God created conflict for a specific purpose.

When God created Adam and Eve, they initially shared life together in the garden where everything was perfect. Both Adam and Eve drew Life directly from God and they looked only to Him to meet their needs (LAWS). As they were drawing life from God they were able to freely share it with each other. Both people drawing a full 100% of their life from God and sharing a full 100% with each other.

In my opinion, the old saying that marriage is 50-50 does not actually describe a good relationship. That type of relationship is what I call the "bank account" relationship. If I make a deposit in your account then I get a withdrawal. If you make a deposit in my account then I let you take a withdrawal. Now don't run home to your spouse and say that Brian said in his book that I don't have to make deposits anymore so I'm not doing all this stuff you make me do just to keep you happy. I'm not saying that we shouldn't be making deposits in others accounts. The problem lies with the idea that something has to be put into the account in order for something to be taken out. Picture this. What if we changed the old saying to marriage is 100-100. Two people fully looking to God to meet their basic needs and then turning to each other to freely share 100% of the love, acceptance, worth, and security. No expectations, no let-downs, no conflict because everyone is always giving. Now I know someone just raised their hand and said, "Now wait a minute Brian, I'm the only one giving and I'm tired of it." We're going to dig into that dilemma in a later chapter and we are going to get very specific.

So let's take a look at a graphic that describes the relationship for Adam, Eve and God and their progression through the fall of man and the loss of communication with God. Why is it that every time I look to another person to meet my needs that I get let down? You're going to love this! When you can actually start to see why you act in a relationship the way you act, we will all start to feel a little less crazy. There is an antidote to the craziness coming soon so don't give up just yet. Let's take a look.

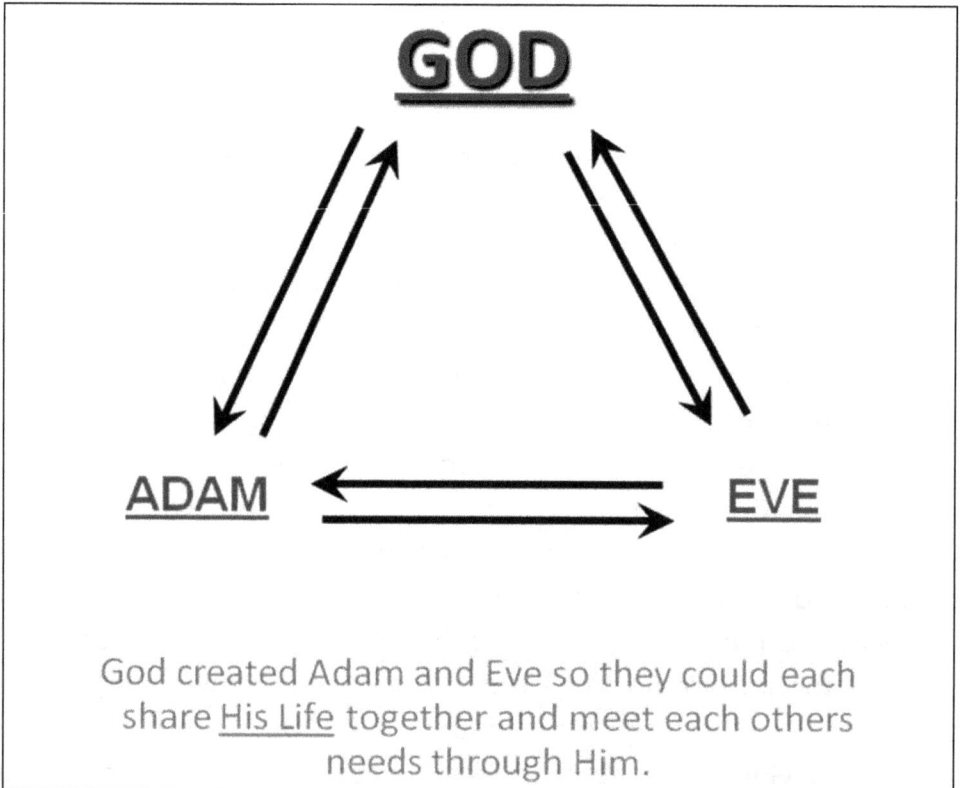

GOD

ADAM ← → EVE

God created Adam and Eve so they could each share His Life together and meet each others needs through Him.

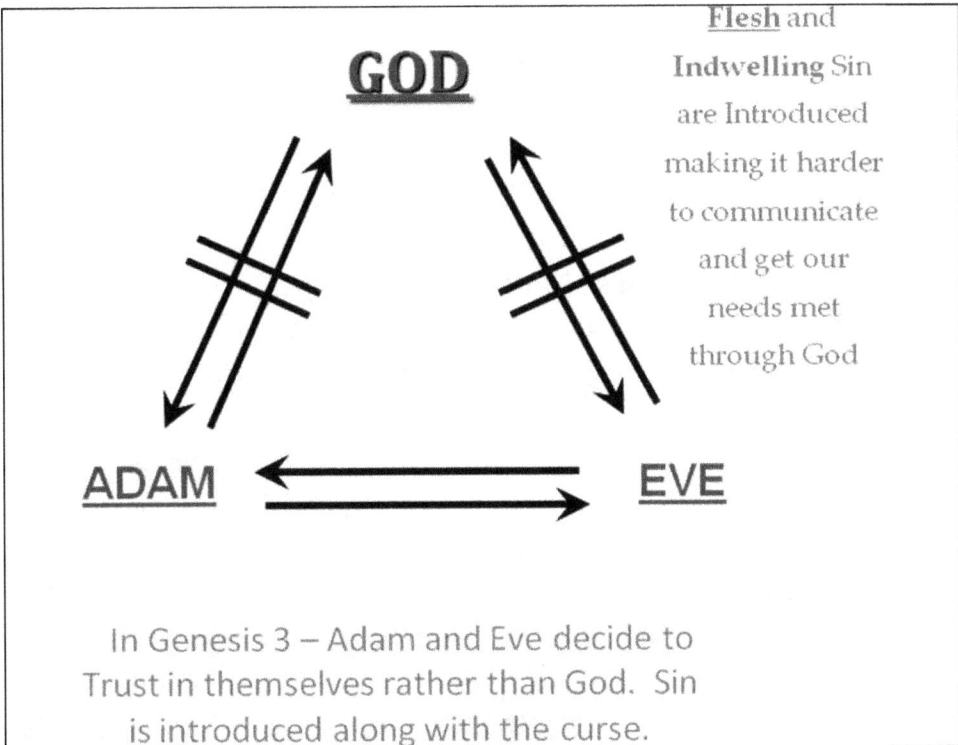

Flesh and Indwelling Sin are Introduced making it harder to communicate and get our needs met through God

In Genesis 3 – Adam and Eve decide to Trust in themselves rather than God. Sin is introduced along with the curse.

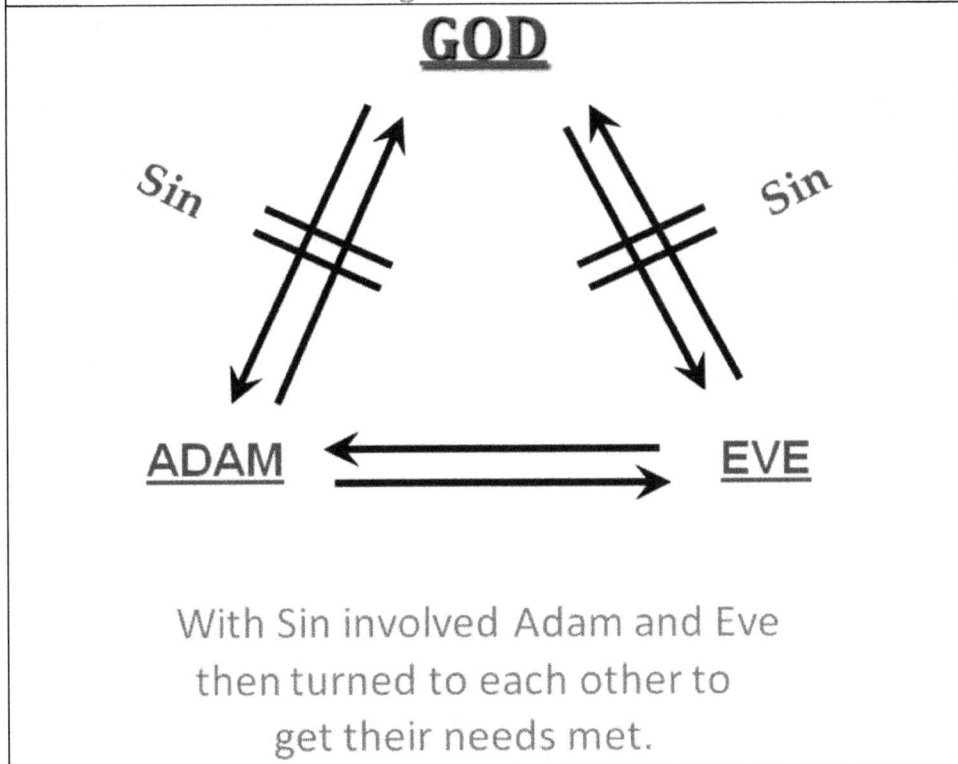

With Sin involved Adam and Eve then turned to each other to get their needs met.

Now here is where it starts to get interesting. Once sin is introduced God has to introduce another plan. Adam and Eve made the decision to meet their own needs instead of looking to God so God provides a plan for the redemption of what had just happened. God still desperately wanted to have the relationship with man so he introduced the curse on man and woman along with his plan to send his Son to redeem the sin and restore the relationship with Him. Let's look a little closer at the curse and see if we can see God's hand of reconciliation at work from the very beginning.

Notice the conflict that God introduced into each relationship. He first introduces conflict into two relationships for the woman. To the woman he said, "*I will make your pains in childbearing very severe; with painful labor you will give birth to children. Your desire will be for your husband, and he will rule over you.*" So here we see conflict added to the relationship between woman and her children and between the woman and her husband. Man is also included in that curse because let's face it, it takes two to tango. Man then receives the curse of trouble in working to provide. To Adam he said, "Cursed is the ground because of you; through painful toil you will eat food from it all the days of your life. It will produce thorns and thistles for you, and you will eat the plants of the field. By the sweat of your brow you will eat your food. That leads us to take a look at our next graph.

GOD

Sin   Sin

Conflict

ADAM ⟵ ⟶ EVE

But sin's curse added conflict between man and woman. It is impossible to meet each others needs outside of God.

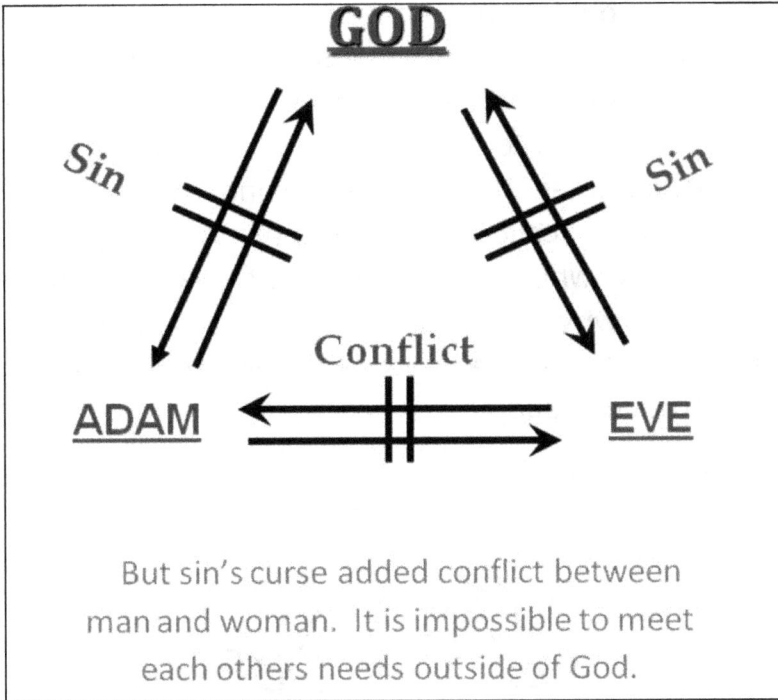

Once man and woman were not meeting each other's needs and they weren't looking to God to meet them, they each had to look somewhere else.

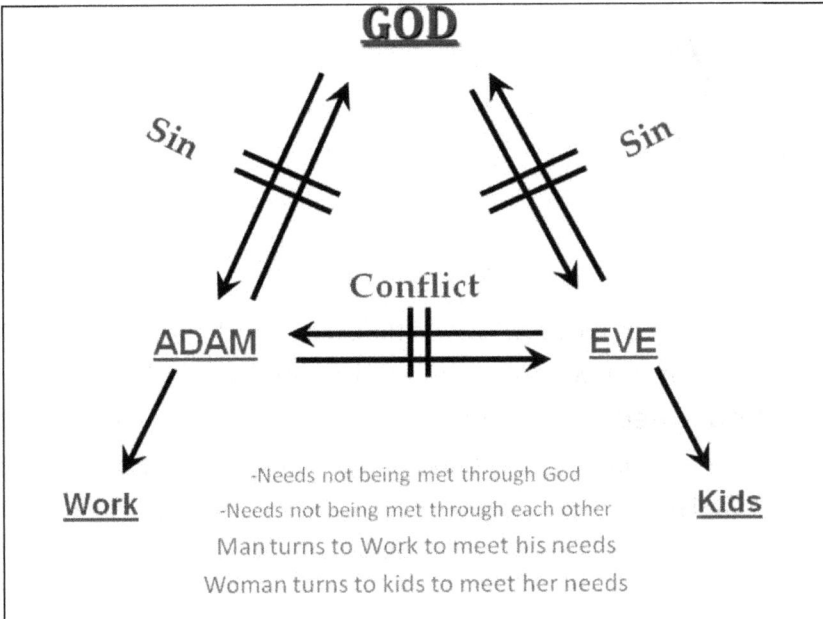

GOD

Sin   Sin

Conflict

ADAM ⟵ ⟶ EVE

Work   Kids

-Needs not being met through God
-Needs not being met through each other
Man turns to Work to meet his needs
Woman turns to kids to meet her needs

When we couldn't get our needs met from our spouse the man turned to work to find L A W S and the woman turned to her kids. Think about how many fractured marriages you have seen where the man is totally focused on work to prove his self-worth and the woman is vicariously living the life she wishes she had through her children. The interesting thing here is that God already knew where we would turn to have our needs met and that may be why he decided to introduce conflict into every relationship with the curse. Notice below what happens when conflict is introduced again.

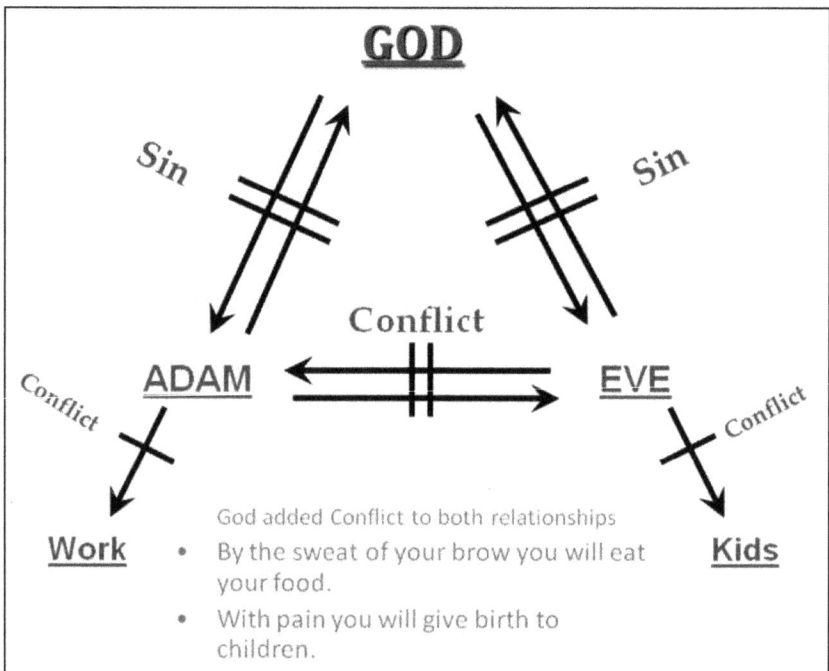

GOD

Sin   Sin

Conflict

Conflict   ADAM ⟵ ‖‖ ⟶ EVE   Conflict

God added Conflict to both relationships

Work   • By the sweat of your brow you will eat your food.   **Kids**

• With pain you will give birth to children.

So why did God add conflict to all these relationships? Could it be that he wanted to be the only one that could ever fully meet our needs? Could it be that all along His plan in adding conflict was to cause us to turn to Him when we failed at finding it anywhere else?

We go through life searching for that magic potion or set of social circumstances that is going to make us happy or give us peace and it just never lasts. We may attain it for a time but there is always that spot deep inside that we know isn't satisfied. A thirst that we can't quite put our finger on or understand but we know it is there. He tells us many times in His word that He is the living water and those who drink of it will never thirst again. He says that He is the peace that passes all understanding. Wouldn't you like to know what it's like to be fully satisfied? To never again have to depend on a flawed human being for love, acceptance worth and security? To be able to freely share those feelings with another person in total freedom with no regret and no guilt? To be completely naked in a beautiful garden and not be ashamed or feel dirty? That my friend is what He is offering. Surrender is not about giving up something. It is about gaining something far more amazing and far more valuable – Total and complete inner peace with who I am and who I was created to be. No expectation to be anything. Just 100% accepted and loved. What if God's plan all along has been for reconciliation of what He lost in the garden? Not what we lost. What He lost. What if I could believe that He desperately wants to love me? Would it change my outlook on life and the way I interact with others? What if He wants to give me the acceptance that no one else on this planet can give? What if He wants to wrap his arms around me and make me feel worthy of his hug?

As you continue in this book we will discuss the process of learning how to take a drink from this not so mystical spring of water. When we finally do reach that water and take a drink from its shores, every relationship will then be available for conflict to be removed. I assume that you would like to remove conflict in your relationships. Well then I have good news because step 1 in the process for starting a new way of living is coming in a few chapters.

Take a look at the final graph that shows a peaceful relationship where we draw life from God and freely give that life to those around us. Seem impractical or hard to imagine? Stay tuned.

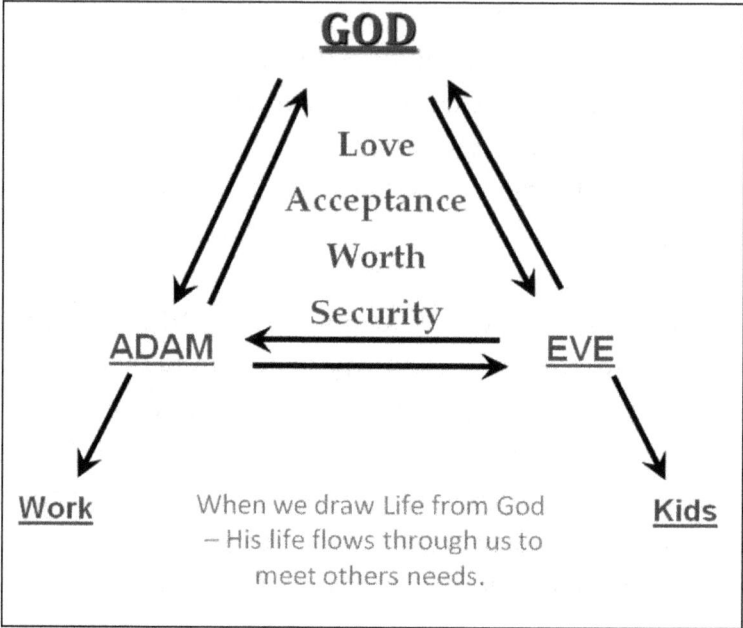

GOD

Love
Acceptance
Worth
Security

ADAM ←→ EVE

Work

When we draw Life from God – His life flows through us to meet others needs.

Kids

Chapter 7
Redemption
The Decapitation of a Soul

"Am I really that bad of a person?" The question from 6 years ago no longer resonated in my mind as I sat in the ice and snow on the highest peak of the house. My arms were wrapped around my knees pulling them tightly to my chest in an attempt to create a little warmth. Now I knew who I was. I was a bad person. I was what they had created me to become. My life was now full of hypocrisy as I attempted to be all things to all people. The lies all seemed to run together. The pain they gave to me, I passed on to others. Any chance to cause pain for someone else seemed to somehow lessen my own. The prophecy proved itself true day after day in my life – "I am a bad person." The hair on my arms stood at attention as the cold was starting to make me shiver.

I had once almost cut off my thumb in a bike accident and my father tried to beat me as I was being taken to the hospital; just because I was so stupid for getting hurt because I didn't listen to his instructions on how to use the bike. This would surely warrant a good beating if I didn't die. Next I thought about the blood that would cover the white snow below. I thought it would be an awesome site to really cover all of that snow with my blood just to show them what they had done to me. But would they really care? Probably not. They didn't seem to care about anybody but themselves.

Many things had happened that brought me to this desperate place of cold solitude. But I couldn't quite forget about last night. No matter how hard I tried to suppress the memory. It held fast and fresh as it played over and over and over. Would death make this memory go away or would it follow me forever in the afterlife as a stinging reminder of how much they hated me? Would it be a reminder of the loveless life lived and tragically thrown away?

Where did it all start? How did I get to the place in my mind where I wanted to die? Why couldn't I just be a normal kid in a normal family?" And that's when it hit me. I wasn't allowed to be a kid. I had to act grown up. Act grown up or suffer the consequences. Suffer as I did at 8 years old. 8 years old – that was the last time I ever remembered crying. The last cry had somehow ripped the tears from my eyes and left them totally barren and dry. And as the snow began to lightly fall in ever so tiny flakes that softly slid off my cheeks and down my arms, no matter how hard I tried, my perfect memory decided to play one of its favorites. An oldie but a 'goodie' as dad always said.

I was 8 years old and as was usual I had to stay late after school waiting for dad to finish work. Dad was the pastor at the church that ran the religious school that I went to. Yes that's right – a for sure enough, Bible thumpin, your all goin to hell if you don't repent preacher man. Preach Jesus during the day – lose your temper and beat your kids at night. But of course this made sense because everything was about performance. And if I didn't perform correctly – well how would that make preacher man look.

I remembered how I used to ask dad how I could help him finish work so we could go home. Dad would tell me to leave him alone so he could finish his work. In the early years I searched for some sort of connection with dad – something that would make dad love me. Really, anything that would bring us together and keep him from beating me. But not now; now I knew I had to stay out of the way; stay hidden as much as possible so as not to give him any extra reasons to lose his temper.

After school I spent most of my time with my only friend in the whole world. A young girl whose father worked at the school was just a year younger than I and lived next door to the school. We would climb the old crabapple tree next to her house and sit there for what seemed like hours swaying in the wind and daring each other to bite into the bitter miniature apples. This was heaven to me. It was my only respite of normalcy in an otherwise chaotic and painful life. She knew nothing about my plight at home and she didn't have to. She was the only person to accept me for who I was. I felt she was the only person in the world that liked me and didn't expect anything from me in return.

The best part of playing in the trees was the wind. I loved the wind. The feeling I had up in a tree was freedom. The wind was free. It came and went as it willed. It was not bound by laws or reason. It didn't have to be a good boy for everyone to love it. It could flex its muscle, show its awe and power, and even throw a temper tantrum and no one could say or do anything about it. What could they do? It's the wind.

I longed to be like the wind. Free from the pull of all the forces that tried to tear me in every direction. "You have to be a better boy Brian. You have to try harder. Do more Brian. You're not doing enough." Up in the trees I couldn't hear any of this. I could only hear the wind as it moved the trees branches slowly back and forth as if rocking a baby to sleep. Hands connected to the tree, the tree connected to the earth, the earth formed by God and pushed gently by his breath. No worries – no cares – just the wind.

But rainy days were bad for me. These days put me into close proximity with dad. And that was not a good place to be. It was on one of these rainy days alone that I was underneath dad's secretary's desk waiting for him to finish work.

Under the desk I had several friends that dad, for some reason, seemed to dislike, but they were my true friends in a lonely world. My first friend was a basketball player. He was about 8 inches tall and made of rubber with wire running through his entire body allowing him to bend in many different positions. His name was Basketball Bob. The second friend was a soccer player named Soccer Joe along with Tennis Pete and Football Frank. Each could be arranged in different formations and positions to provide entertainment and help pass the alone time. I would spend hours talking to my friends and creating impossible scenarios of doom and gloom only to have the fantastic foursome of sports heroes show up to save the day.

And then without provocation or warning the unthinkable happened. Basketball Bob, Soccer Joe, Tennis Pete, and Football Frank were all brutally and senselessly murdered.

It all started with dad walking into the office and for what seemed to be without reason he announced that I was too old to be playing with dolls. "They are not dolls dad, they are my friends." I retorted a little sarcastically. Then in one fell swoop and with much resistance from me, dad wrestled all of the rubber wire friends away. I begged for him to give them back as I jumped up and down wildly attempting to grab them back. Then it happened all so fast. It was unconscionable and horrifying. "How could this be happening" I wondered. But it was happening. The scissors were in dads hand and headed for the neck of Basketball Bob. He laughed heartily and with great joy as he squeezed the scissors handles. Bob's head shot up off of his body and straight up into the air. My eyes watched in horror as Bob's head flew through the air and then bounced across the floor coming to a stop just a few inches from my right foot.

I didn't know what to think. I didn't know what to feel. Everything had always been done to me but now it was being

56

done to one of my friends and I was powerless to do anything about it. I fantasized about turning into the Incredible Hulk. "If I was David Banner I would turn into The Hulk right now and tear him to pieces!" And then, one by one, each of the four sports heroes were beheaded. Each head flying up violently into the air and then bouncing around on the ground as if screaming in pain, before rolling to a slow painful stop.

Of course as traumatized as I was at this moment it all had to be summed up in one final phrase from dad. It seemed he always had to give us something to walk away with or some explanation as to why this horrible decapitation had to take place. The words came quickly from his mouth but seemed to me as if they were in slow motion. Like when David Banner was being tormented right before his change from normal person into animalistic rage. Everything slowed for effect. The pain had to be delivered in order for The Incredible Hulk to show up. And then he said the words that would change the course of my life for many years to come. "Grow Up! You're too old to play with dolls."

Grow up. I pondered the words that had been so rudely and abruptly spoken as dad walked out of the room. As he left, I crawled back under the desk and began to cry. Tears of hurt, disgust, and confusion turned slowly to tears of rage. These are the tears that are hot and burn with malevolence as they roll down your cheeks. There was nothing healing or calming about these tears.

Tears of rage turned quickly to no tears. No tears turned to the beginning of a cold and dark indifference. Those soft, child-like, mischievous, hazel eyes began to harden as they filled with rage and hatred of everyone and everything. It would be another 27 years before another real tear flowed out of those once soft and warm hazel eyes.

What has someone spoken into your life that you have internalized as truth? I wish that there were classes for parents that would teach them the impact that their words have on children. I wish that there where classes for husbands and wives that taught them the impact of what they say to each other. How long does someone have to hear that they are useless and stupid before they start to believe it? Did someone tell you that you were too messed up to be loved? Worse yet, did you believe it to the point that it is now part of who you are and affects how you live your life?

One of the hardest lies to break for me was either seeing me or everyone around me as idiots. I kept the bar set really high and expected excellence from everyone. It really wasn't even excellence that I expected. It was really that I wanted it done my way. Once I realized that this was a recurring phrase in my head I thought back to childhood and remembered where it came from. Both dad and grandpas favorite phrase upon completing any project was "Not too bad for a dummy." No wonder I was always trying to overachieve and putting others down for not living up to the standard I had set. I had begun to live my life trying to overcome this one phrase.

Your homework is to spend 30 minutes writing down things that someone has spoken into your life that may not be true. These things may be hard to pinpoint because you may really see them as truth. Close your eyes in a quiet place and they will come to you. They won't come in all at once and may even come in over the course of a few years. No need to rush this process though. Take the time and let it happen as it happens. There may be one giant lie that covers many other lies but you can deal with them as they are revealed to you. Believe me, you and your mental health are worth the time that you will put into this exercise.

Chapter 8
Revelation

Control – Illusion or Reality?

As I mentioned before, I love being given steps to any process. An outline, instructions, directions – It doesn't really matter what you want to call them. Without the manual for the furniture in the box from IKEA, it's just a box full of wood and some funny looking screws and bolts. So let's begin to break down what it is that keeps us from finding peace and introduce some new ways of thinking that can help us move on to the next step in the process.

Let's go back to our definition of surrender from the dictionary. Webster actually gives 4 definitions:

    A. To yield to the power, possession or control of another.
    B. To give up completely or agree to forgo especially in favor of another.
    C. To give (oneself) up into the power of another.
    D. To give (oneself) over to something.

When asking groups of people to define what they think surrender means the most common responses are – to give up, to let go, to give everything to God. All decent responses but the root questions have to be "What am I giving up? What am I letting go of? What am I giving to God and why do I even need to give it?" The best way to answer these questions is to take a look at our lives and try to see if we can recognize what it is that we really are holding on to so tightly. What is it that keeps us feeling safe at night and makes us feel warm and fuzzy? What is it that when we don't think we have it, it makes our worlds spiral into fret, worry and frustration? The short 7 letter answer – Control. This tiny little word is what everything is riding on and it all began before we were even here with Lucifer. Now I'm not going to attempt to say the devil made me do it and blame everything on him. I just want to travel down a path that can help us see how he has used people that we trust to affect how we think and believe.

When Lucifer led the choir in heaven and looked around he thought he could do just a little bit better. He believed that he was a little more talented and that if just given the chance he could do it his way and he could be... that's right... in control. Well we all know how that turned out. It turns out he really wasn't as in control or powerful as he thought. It turns out that nobody is more powerful than the Almighty and Lucifer was cast out of heaven.

But he wasn't alone. One third of the angels in heaven went with him. What this means is that Lucifer was a good salesperson. I guess we really can't even say good. Heck, he is a great salesperson! He has a conversion rate of 1 out of 3.

So now you ask, Brian, why are we talking about the sales skills of the devil? As usual, I'm so glad you asked. There are several reasons. First, know your opponent. If we are truly locked in a life and death battle for our mind and our souls than doesn't it make sense to know who your opponent is and what his goals are? Of course it does. This fiend is the ultimate deceiver and he is in it to win it. All he has to do is plant a few core lies into your mind and you could live out the rest of your life believing that you are a failure and that you'll never amount to anything. Or you may believe that you are too smart and powerful to believe in God, too self-sufficient and don't need anyone else, or... you fill in the blank. What's your lie? What bill of goods has he sold you on? His only job is to sell you on who you're not. I hope you picked up on that. In case you didn't I'll write it again and this time you can underline it. His only job is to make you believe that you are someone that you are not. Through my experience I have come to believe that God created each of us with a specific goal and a purpose. God tells us in both Jeremiah and Psalms "Before I formed you in the womb I knew you". The deceiver's goal is to come in when we are young and impressionable and plant a seed of doubt. He is very clever with this process. If he came straight out and told you that the sky was green, who would believe him? The trick is to take the truth and twist it just enough so it becomes a lie that still looks a little bit like the truth. A lie that is very easy to believe because it is so closely related to the truth. Take for instance the serpents lie to Eve in the Garden of Eden. Are you sure that's what God said? Are you sure that's what he meant? Well, what if he actually meant this?

To carry that even further, Paul mentioned in the first chapter of Romans that many of us will end up serving the creature more than the creator because the truth of God was changed into a lie. And who is the creature? That's right. It's us. We end up worshipping ourselves. This might be a tough pill for some of us to swallow but I have discovered that changes in my life cannot take place without swallowing that pill. We are going to have to take a painful look inward and notice that most of my life has been lived for me. But let's not swallow that pill just yet. We're going to leave it on the counter and stare at it for a while.

Now once the deceiver has planted the seed of a lie in us, as we grow he waters it and uses circumstances in our life to make sure that we continue to believe the lie and spread it to others... even our children. I'm getting ahead of myself. We'll get back to that later.

The second reason we want to take notice of Lucifer's skills is to have the realization that he uses other unsuspecting sales people to unknowingly lead us down the wrong path. If Lucifer was able to deceive one third of the entire host of heaven, how many deceived people do you think are here on this earth. It seems that many times well-meaning people have been sold false information by the great deceiver and then they re-sell it as the truth. This "truth" may come from someone we trust and hold in high regard. It could be a parent, favorite teacher, pastor or mentor. No one is above being sold a lie.

Many times along my journey I have in my mind been 100% certain about how I saw God and the world. I have been adamant to the point of wanting to burn my opponents at the stake for heresy, only to realize 6 months later that I have a different view of God. The funny part was that once I adopted the new view I again became a champion on a crusade for the new view. The problem then becomes, How do I know which of my beliefs are lies and which of them are the truth? Now that's a great question and this is really the fun part – Question everything! As a child, most of us had everyone telling us what to believe and exactly how to believe it. As an adult the responsibility for my spirituality now belongs to me. If I choose to go on this spiritual journey for complete and total peace in my heart, mind and soul than I have to question everything that I have ever been taught and scrub it against the truth.

That then leads us to ask, "So where do I find the Truth?" As soon as you hear that question I'll bet you're ready for me to throw out one of the old standards of religion and say that all you have to do is read the Bible. Well I'm going to go off the reservation here and disagree. While I believe the Bible is filled with Truth and that it is a great source to find principles and guidance for our lives, it can also be used out of context to lead anyone astray. If I gave a passage from the Bible to several different people they would most likely come back to me with different explanations of what it means with each one basing their findings on their own personal bent. The problem is that the words in the Bible rely on man's interpretation and our interpretation can be skewed based on how we grew up, who our mentors are, and if we have yet learned to hear the leading of the Holy Spirit. In this chapter we are addressing the first two. Hearing the voice of the Holy Spirit comes once we have learned to let go, so we will address that a little later down the road.

Consider this. Because of our innate desire to be accepted, many people will assimilate to their surroundings as they grow up. If someone grows up with parents that are Catholic and conservative, what religion and political view are they most likely to have. Even if they don't attend a church they may go through the rest of their life believing and telling others that they are a Catholic. But the point here is that the only reason this person believes this about themselves is because that is what they grew up in. They could just as easily have grown up in a barn and believed they were a farmer.

The most important part here is to look for any belief planted in our mind, heart, and soul from our upbringing that defines who we believe we are. These beliefs can be planted by any person of influence so be sure to question everything. Remember, this process is about learning who the person deep down inside of us is and that person is most likely covered by years of beliefs that are ready to be questioned. A good friend of mine named Michele calls this process unraveling. Because once you discover a lie that exists at the core level in your life then you have to see how many areas of your life are affected. The lie can branch out from the core to affect every area and every relationship.

So if I can't yet find the truth in the Bible than how do I find the truth? The good news is that you don't have to find the truth. When you embark on this journey and take the steps laid out in front of you in this book then the Truth will find you. You will hear it and feel it in every fiber of who you are. You will find it in the dark and know that it is the truth the same way that you know how to find the bathroom in the middle of the night with the lights off. This may sound cryptic now but it will start to make sense in a few more chapters. Stick with me. We'll get there. "And you will know the Truth and the Truth will set you free."

Let's talk a little bit more about control. Did you think I was gonna let you off the hook on that one? Let's dig a little deeper into that thing that we think we have – control. I'm sure many of us may have heard the old saying at one time or another that control is an illusion. This is very easy to say for someone who is out of control but for those who are in control it is easy to truly believe that I am orchestrating every minute detail throughout my daily schedule. With the idea that I am in control comes the concept that I am calling all the shots. Where do you think the phrase 'God complex' comes from? When I am calling all of the shots then I am in charge of creating my life and my destiny. Let's see if I can make this a little clearer by quoting a young brash man that I used to know named Brian. This is the speech he used to give to anyone who came into his office and complained about anything. "I grew up in hell and I decided that I was going to get out. I got my first job at age 8 and worked hard. I grabbed myself by my bootstraps and pulled myself out and made something of myself."

This causes me to pose a question. Who is God in Brian's life? God never had a chance to be God to Brian because Brian was firmly entrenched on the throne in his life. Of course I am talking about myself and I did finally ask God to be king of my life. What I wasn't prepared for was the part where He had to forcefully remove me from His throne. You're gonna love that story when we get to it! Can't wait to tell it!

So why is it we believe we are in control anyway? Does anyone want to take a guess at how fast we are moving through the universe right now? At the equator the earth is rotating at about 1,000 MPH. The Earth is also revolving around the sun at around 66,000 MPH. Our solar system is moving around the center of our galaxy at approximately 420,000 MPH. All that added up is 487,000 MPH but just wait, it gets even better. There is speculation that the galaxy is moving through the universe at a speed of 2,237,000 MPH. When we add that up it turns out that instead of just sitting here reading this book and believing that you are totally in control, you are moving at a speed of 2.7 million miles per hour right now. All it takes is one tiny cosmic speed bump and we might fall out of our seats, or worse yet, off the edge of the galaxy.

So if we start to digest the idea that we're not actually in control and we develop the desire to attain a new level of peace in life then where do we start? Great question! Let's start by doing some homework. To do your homework you're going to need a journal. Journaling is a major key to making life changes. Journaling allows the subconscious to communicate with the conscious by pulling out what you are thinking and re-introducing it to your mind through the eyes. You will most likely be surprised at the accelerated growth you will experience when you start this simple exercise. Journaling can be done when you wake up or when you go to bed depending on when your mind is most acute and awake. Journaling is really as simple as writing down specific thoughts and feelings that you are having throughout the day. It should consist of around 15 minutes of time spent somewhere quiet. I know that sounds scary to those of us who are used to constant noise and distraction but I promise you that once you start doing it, not only will you love it but you will start to attain a new clarity within your thought process. Just seeing your thoughts and feelings on paper can give a certain sense of validity when needed or completely render powerless the lies that are screaming in your mind.

Another exercise in journaling is to list at the end of each day the questions that you have for God and then get really quiet and ask Him what questions He has for you. Just write down the things that come to your mind no matter how bizarre you think they are.

We can also begin a process that I like to call Holy Spirit Inventory. It can be easy for me to take inventory of my life and write down the things that I like and the things that I want and don't want. But introducing the Holy Spirit and giving him permission to walk through our thoughts and feelings can accelerate the process of unraveling what is going on in our minds. Call it inner thought, a conscience, or whatever you like. Ultimately the Holy Spirit is there to guide our thought life and lead us towards Christ. If the voice you hear is condemning you, than it is not the Holy Spirit. It is the great deceiver. Remember that his job is to tell you who you are not. You have to learn to reject the voice that condemns you and accept the voice that comforts you and compels you to want to be a better person. The Holy Spirit never condemns us. He only approaches us with true guilt as he holds us in his arms and reminds us that we messed up but He still loves us and wants to redeem us. Satan and his tormentors use false guilt that condemns us and tells us things like "You'll never be good enough. You'll never make up for all you've done. You screwed up again you big idiot." The easy way to remember this is that the Holy Spirit is compelling with love and Satan is condemning. I almost hate to say that it is as simple as the old Bugs Bunny cartoon with the devil on one shoulder and the angel on the other. But the battle for our mind can be just that simple. As I continue my personal story you will see that condemning self-talk that I used to believe was the voice of God himself condemning me. The more you practice listening and journaling the more you will begin to differentiate between the two sources.

Once you have your journal we can start by asking ourselves these three questions in an attempt to find out where our search for surrender starts.

1. What are the things that I am holding onto very tightly?

Ask the Holy Spirit to bring specifics to your mind. This is not the time to be general.

2. Where am I getting the four needs met? Identify each of the four areas and where I am looking in each category.

3. What am I using to define myself? Am I looking to a job, hobby, clothing style, kids, church, childhood or relationship to define who I am? Be real with yourself and spend the time necessary to come up with the answers from the Holy Spirit.

We also need to keep in mind that it is important as we read and journal not to underline for someone else. Some people read a book and turn down the corners of a page and highlight certain sections and then hand the book to their spouse and say "Here, I found some things for you to apply in your life." Well gee, thanks. This journey is for you and only you. I can tell you about so many times that I tried to apply what I was learning to someone else and it ended badly. Each person is accountable to God for their relationship with Him and God does it in His timing and not in ours. How many times have you tried to be the Holy Spirit in someone else's life and how did that work out for you? Has someone else tried to be the Holy Spirit for you and how did you feel? Most likely you rebelled. Everything is up to God's timing and God's control.

This exercise will most likely take longer than the usual journaling session. So challenge yourself to go deep as you ask yourself some important questions that have the ability to change how you see the world and how you see yourself.

Chapter 9
Redemption

Growing Up Fast – The Money Trap

And so I did what it was I was asked to do. I grew up. I stopped playing with toys and started working. Any work I could find I was on it. It didn't matter what it was as long as it paid and kept me out of the house. Bailing hay with the farmer was always fun work but then I landed my first real job with an employer. The school was looking for a janitorial assistant and so my older brother and I took the job. $20 dollars a week for 3 hours of work a day. And so the toys went into the closet and I set out to learn how to be all grown up. The more money I made the more I started to like money. Money was awesome! Money provided some sort of freedom. If I had enough perhaps I could be completely free from my parents. If I had my own money perhaps I wouldn't need them at all.

I looked for every opportunity I could to earn money. Cutting grass, washing windows, cleaning cars and bailing hay all took the place of play. There was no longer any time to climb trees. I now longed for a different type of freedom. The wind wasn't going to take me anywhere but this money sure was. Money was definitely the answer to all of my problems. If I could only get enough I would be completely free.

As the money flowed in I felt a great sense of accomplishment. I also felt so empowered by the ability to spend focused time and energy toward a specific cause and the end result of being paid for a job well done. I learned to take pride in a job well done and began to focus on perfection. Everything had to be done perfectly. Small abnormalities in anything began to bother me. If it wasn't perfectly straight, perfectly cut, or perfectly cleaned it was a problem that would not go away until it was corrected.

It always seemed that I was the only member of my family looking for some sort of order amidst the chaos. I was laughed at and belittled for my sense of cleanliness and order. My room was perfection – everything in order and everything in its place. The rest of the house was cluttered and disorderly. I would spend hours cleaning and organizing the garage just the way I liked it. I was always looking for that one small piece of affirmation from anybody at all. "Great job Brian, what an amazing job." But I only received ridicule for being such a freak.

Customers seemed to love my devotion to perfection though. Their yards were cut cleanly and manicured to a tee. Their cars and windows were spotless and streak free. Of course it takes more time to do something right, but I had nothing but time. Every hour spent working was an hour away from home and a chance to get more of what I loved – money. And money gave me what I craved most – freedom. But this perceived freedom turned out to be short lived.

I was not very frugal with my money. Yes I did save some, but it was usually so I could buy something I wanted. I would set a goal for myself and then work till I had the money to buy what I wanted and then spend it. The candy store also got its fair share of my money, but much of it went towards my favorite activity – eating.

I was not a true professional at eating but if there was a contest, or better yet, a double dog dare, I was up for the challenge. Two piled high plates of pasta – three sloppy joe sandwiches – a foot long burrito – no matter what the menu, I went all out. I had a metabolism that most people would kill for. I ate all I wanted and never gained weight. At Thanksgiving dinner everyone would sit and watch in amazement as I would polish off my fourth plate of food. "Where are you putting all that food" they would remark. "Do you have a hollow leg?" I once put an entire Whopper in my mouth all at once and swallowed it, just on a dare.

In 4th grade I sold the most candy during the school fund raiser and won the right to go to McDonalds and order whatever I wanted. I ordered a Big Mac, a Quarter Pounder with cheese, a 20 piece box of Chicken Nuggets, a Filet-O-Fish sandwich, 2 large fries, a cherry pie, and a hot fudge sundae with nuts. It took about 30 minutes for me to finish it all. The crowd clapped and cheered as the last bite of hot fudge sundae rolled off the spoon and into my completely full stomach. I won this challenge every year because not only could I eat, but I was a masterful salesperson.

I got the gift of selling from my father. Dad could sell anything. No matter what dad said, people were buying. I learned the skill of smooth talking and the ever so subtle art of manipulation. The key to manipulation is to let others feel they are in charge and that every idea is their idea. Dad didn't know it, but he had a young apprentice watching his every move and learning how to sell, manipulate, and worst of all, how to be angry.

But as usual, the parental units just had to get involved in my business. As they noticed the small fortune I had amassed for someone my age and the independence I was gaining, they somehow felt it was time to reign me in. They told me they didn't like how I was spending my money and tried to tell me what I should be doing with my money. None of their suggestions were to my liking so I did what he always did. I spoke my mind. You would think that after years of being beaten that I would have been broken by now. Broken into submission to do and say what I was told. But not me – my will to challenge the norm and have my questions answered still reigned supreme. "It's my money, I earned it, and I can spend it however I want."

The declaration was bold and intended to make a statement. It was sort of a line in the sand kind of moment for me. They had infringed on my life in so many areas but they were not going to tell me what I could do with my hard earned money. But tell me they did. After a good old fashioned beating for my insolence to the king and queen, all money for all jobs was now to be paid directly to them. They were now to choose how much I could have, where I could go to spend it, and what I could spend it on.

I didn't know what to feel. "How could they do this? They have no right to take my money." I fumed quietly as I knew to say anything would not change the situation or help in any way. To say more might incur more pain. I would take the pain if I knew I could have my money. But the warlords had spoken and the gavel had been slammed down ever so violently as judgment was pronounced.

Back on the rooftop, my freedom was in a precarious position teetering on the edge of doubt. "Will I ever have a chance to be free". "It's my money, I earned it. You can't take it from me." "It's my money, I earned it. I can do whatever I want with it." I held my hands tightly over my ears as I tried to keep from hearing the words playing over and over again in my crystal clear memory. I've been up here for a while now. Do they even know I'm missing? Do they even care? Will they care if I don't come back at all?

Your homework for this chapter is to evaluate your relationship with money. Money was what I turned to for self-worth and security. What do you look to money for? Does it control you? Do you control it? One of the most impactful questions that I have ever heard about money came from Andy Stanley. Which of the following would impact your life and your feelings more? If you woke up in the morning and found out that your bank account was empty or if you woke up and found out that there was no God. Is money the god you go to for security and self-worth?

Now we're not going to deal with this just yet. We just want to write down our thoughts on money as it relates to us. We will discuss dealing with redefining the relationship in a later chapter.

Chapter 10
Revelation
Bad Habits

Once we decide that we would like to make changes in our lives there are several different directions we can go in. One of the most popular directions that many people head into is to try to fix all of the problems in their life by focusing on cleaning up all of their bad habits. These are usually habits that have developed over the years and someone has consistently pointed them out to us, and so we begin the process of trying to fix all of the little things that will make me look like a better person. Maybe we try to give up our addictions, quell our anger, or identify some past bitterness that we would like to remove. I myself spent the first five years of my spiritual life fighting this uphill battle.

Please hear me when I say that this is a mountain that cannot be conquered and ends only in despair and intense spiritual warfare. Maybe you have been there. Maybe you have been on that religious treadmill that keeps you running and fighting for righteousness. As you keep running on this treadmill, it continually repeats the phrase, "The better I am the more God will love me and the more I do the more I am accepted." We get off the treadmill and notice that we haven't gotten anywhere in our spiritual life and so we rededicate ourselves, do more and work harder.

There is actually a fundamental flaw with the act of attempting to attain righteousness that I think you will find very interesting. Either you fail in the attempt and condemn yourself for not being able to live up to the standard that you have set for yourself; or you live up to the standard that you have set for yourself and condemn everyone else for not being able to live up to that standard. It is a lose-lose scenario.

The reality is that our habits are just surface symptoms of a deeper issue. It's kind of like having an illness that has symptoms like fatigue, joint pain and skin rashes and then trying to treat each of the symptoms instead of looking for the cause. You can put medicated lotion on the rash, inject cortisone into the joint, lose weight and exercise to help the fatigue but at the end of the day if you don't treat the cancer that is causing the symptoms then you are just going to continue to get sicker.

Now the interesting thing to note is that when you treat a symptom it can actually get better for a time or even be totally eradicated by monitoring behavior. But treating a symptom is kind of like cutting off the leg of an octopus. The other legs just get stronger. We work for weeks and even months to make one bad habit go away only to find out that another one has gotten stronger. To kill an octopus you have to go for the head. You must find the disease at the source of the symptoms. But the question is "What is at the head of the octopus?" What is it that is always fighting against me and thwarting my attempts at living a peaceful life? The answer is given to us by Paul in Romans 5-8. In these chapters Paul is laying out his heart and sharing the battle that exists in the mind between him wanting to do good but then somehow the flesh ends up causing him to do what he doesn't want to do. So what is this flesh that Paul is talking about? Well, let's take a look at a concept that has the potential to change your life as it adjusts the way that you will think about the flesh and sin from this point forward. I struggled for many years trying to figure out what Paul was talking about in this passage. I even fell victim to the lie that says that I might as well go ahead and sin because I have no control over my flesh and I will be forgiven anyway. This way of thinking kept me on a roller coaster back and forth between condemnation and forgiveness for quite some time. That was until I gained a new understanding of what Paul was saying in this passage.

When Paul uses the word sin in Romans 5-8 the form of the word is not a verb. It is a noun. This changes sin in this passage from being an action that I commit to being an entity that is alive and inside of me. That means that inside of me is something that was left by Adam's sin in the Garden of Eden. We can call this several different things. We can call it the flesh, indwelling sin, or just simply the voice in my head that condemns me and leads me in the direction of pain and sadness. As much as the Holy Spirit wants to lead us towards peace and happiness, this evil force wants to lead us toward destruction and ruin. For a greater understanding of Romans 5-8 read Watchman Nee's book The Normal Christian Life. It truly is the textbook that should accompany this passage of scripture. The goal at this point is just to understand that there are two voices that exist inside of me. Once is there to lead me to peace and the other is there to lead me to ruin.

A few chapters ago we discussed the process of starting to learn how to tell the difference between the two voices. What we want to make sure we understand now is that we can have victory over all of our habits by going directly to the disease. The tentacles of the octopus are bothersome to deal with but they are just symptoms of the real issue of the flesh and its fight for control in our lives. The flesh is the head of the octopus and is cancerous. Let's take a look at a graphic that shows us what it looks like to fight the octopus.

Flesh is like an Octopus

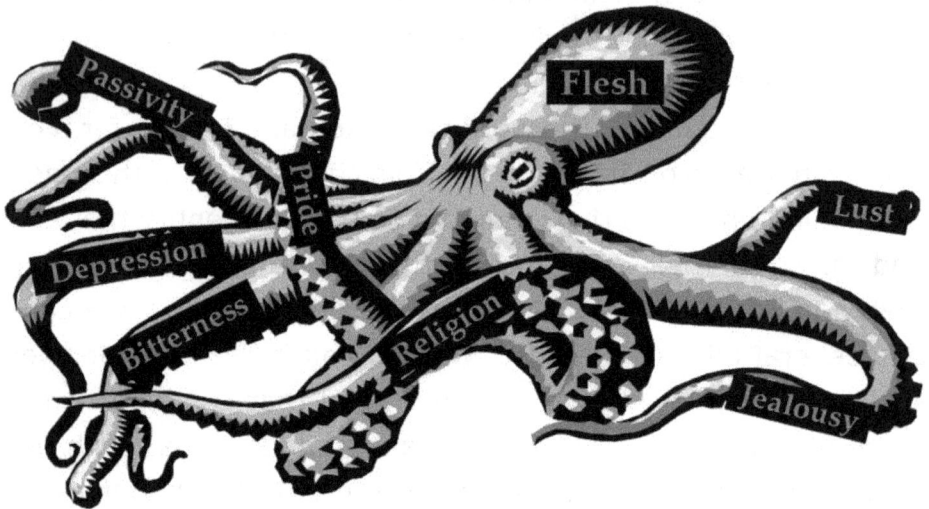

Passivity

Pride

Flesh

Lust

Depression

Bitterness

Religion

Jealousy

So what is the Flesh? The Flesh is the condition (*mindset, attitude, strategy of living*) in which my primary focus is on myself, leading me to live out of my own resources (*such as humor, talents, education, looks, or self-discipline*) in order to:

1. Cope with my life
2. Solve my problems
3. Meet my needs
4. Become a success

In short, living in the flesh is me choosing to live my own life the way I see best in my control to get my needs met.

The core desire of the flesh is really to be in control. When you wake up in the morning your first thought is generally about you and what you want to accomplish to meet your needs today or it is about how someone else upset you by not meeting your needs. That leads you to deciding how you are going to act towards that person today so that you can be sure that they know that you are hurt by their sub-par performance and you will be upset for the remainder of the day/week or until they do something to make your mood better. Sound familiar? Are you the king or queen of the silent treatment? Well, he should know what kind of idiot he is and that he hurt me and I'm not telling him till he figures it out. Are you tired of living this way? There is another way but it starts with surrendering two core items in the arena of control. First is my control of my life and second is my control of those around me.

The best place to start may be to first identify how it is that you attempt to control things in your life and those around you. Are you aggressive or passive aggressive? Do you confront every situation head on with a fiery intensity or did the silent treatment scenario strike a nerve?

I remember a counselor pointing out to me that I would gladly fight my way across 20 lanes of downtown highway traffic if I thought that there was a good argument to be had on the other side. My spouse, however, would be on the other side calmly declaring with a stern face that nothing was wrong but that if something were wrong then I should certainly know what it was that I had done.

So what is your method of control? Do you expect others to read your mind and know what you are feeling? What are the games that you play in your attempt at manipulating others to get your needs met? Who are the people that you attempt to control? Go ahead and make some notes in your journal about your methods of control and where you would like to let go of some control in an attempt to procure peace.

What are the bad habits that are at the top of your list that you usually work on? Make a list of each of them and then link each of them back to the head of the octopus. Is each one an attempt to get your perceived needs met in some way? Is it really all about you? Go ahead and make your lists and we will talk more about how to let go of some of that control later.

Chapter 11
Redemption
Alone on the Edge of Eternity

It has been said that children are the best recorders of information and the worst interpreters. When I was 4, I remember being on a road trip in the car with the whole family. My older brother kept begging dad to find a bathroom because he had to go so bad. As dad looked for a place to stop my brother rolled down his window and began to vomit out of the car! Now while that is something that I will never forget I want you to notice how my mind interpreted the event. After viewing that event I believed that if you had to go to the bathroom really bad and you waited too long... That's right, it will come up and out the other end! Let me tell you. Every time I had to go to the bathroom for the next 5 years I was very adamant about finding one quickly because I didn't want that in my mouth! My interpretation of the event led to a belief that wasn't true, which then led to a new way to live my life.

As I sat out in the cold on the edge of eternity my mind continued playing all of the recordings that I wished would go away never to be seen again. But my interpretation of every event was what did most of the damage in my persona and who I became. "I am a bad boy" I would hear in my mind. "I am no good for anyone – Nobody loves me – I must not be very lovable – I will never be good enough so why should I try."

Why try seemed to be the prevailing theme. Nothing was ever good enough. Because mom was always sick and dad was always at work, I had to learn to take care of myself. Cooking, cleaning, laundry, and the usual upkeep of the property was all the responsibility of us boys. Mom did what she could but her illness kept her on the sidelines.

Mom was also very confused. She bought into the lie of righteousness and attempted to keep us all living on the straight and narrow. The lie of righteousness tells us that it is our responsibility to please God by creating high moral standards for ourselves and then adhering to them in an attempt to appease and please God. Talk about living in a pressure cooker. We were always one slip up away from landing in the hot seat. And the hot seat was never a good, or fun, place to be.

It usually occurred after any type of infraction whether minor or major. The feared, ominous words could be heard and would echo as if in slow motion as the mind wondered if it had actually heard them. "Go to your room and wait for your father to get home." I felt that this was where I spent most of my life. Time seemed to stop and the hours slowly whittled away as I waited for the pain to arrive. To prepare for the pain several extra pairs of underwear would be added and the thickest pair of blue jeans available would be worn.

The worst part was always the waiting. Wondering what kind of mood he would be in. Wondering how long it would last. Would he be tired and want to get it over with and go to bed, or angry and want to prolong the pain just to, somehow alleviate his own.

But the events of last night were much different. Last night the proverbial you know what didn't just hit the fan, it exploded and flew in every corner and crevice of the room and then was left to rot, fester, and seep into a damaged soul.

The day trudged along as any other but quickly took a turn for the worse as mom walked in on a conversation between my younger brother and I as we were fighting over whose turn it was to play our new video game. I loved the new video game. Grandpa had bought the family 'Pong' - the first video game ever. It was always a lot of fun. But this new system, the Atari 2600 was the gaming system of the future. So many games and so many places to take your mind away from what was going on in the real world.

I excelled at video games. I had the high score on every game we owned. Others would watch in amazement and wonder how I avoided destruction at every turn by a fraction of a second only to turn the tables and defeat the bad guys. If only eating a Power Pellet would help me defeat my demons. One magical, glowing ball of light to turn the tables and your enemies are running from you like scared chickens. If only it were that easy.

As I played my younger brother continued to pester me insisting over and over again that it was his turn to play. But I was on a roll. Once a world record score was set in motion I couldn't be stopped. All focus was set intently on every jump, slide, or turn. "Don't touch me" I would holler, "You'll mess me up."

My brother should've known better. I once threw a controller at him when he messed me up and knocked his front tooth right out of his mouth. My rage was becoming less hidden and seeping out into every relationship around me.

But still, he wouldn't leave me alone. "Don't touch me – Leave me alone - You can play when I'm finished." I shouted. The words didn't seem all that harsh to me and they didn't sound any different than the words that were always shouted at me. But mom was growing more and more tired of my independent attitude. She thought I acted as if I didn't need anyone else. I was rude and insensitive to everyone unless it served my purpose to be otherwise. I was downright rebellious and rebellion could not be tolerated. Next thing I knew she was shouting my name I knew what was coming. "Go to your room and wait for your father to get home." I walked to my room, closed the door behind me, and turned and shook my fist in rage as I sat down for the long wait.

It was preached in church that rebellion was the root of all evil and must be stopped at all costs and through any means necessary. But I didn't care what they preached anymore. None of it really made any sense. I was told at a young age that if I sinned that God would strike me dead with a bolt of lightning or put worms in my stomach to eat me from the inside out. Or better yet, just open up the ground beneath me to swallow me whole down into the fiery pits of hell.

But rebellion questions everything and decides to put it to the test. After being beaten day after day how's a little lightning going to scare me. I even welcomed a bolt of lightning or the earth to swallow me whole. It would bring an end to the onslaught of pain and suffering that was my life.

And so I began to test them and God at every turn. A once well behaved somewhat mischievous boy began to turn into what they created – a Bad Boy. The infractions started out as small. If you're going to test an all-powerful God there's no sense in starting with capital crimes. After realizing that I was still alive after each journey to the dark side I would smile as if to say "I told you so."

I became emboldened by my new discoveries. "If God doesn't kill me over the small things, maybe I can do whatever I want." And so another lie began to grow in the foundation of my mind. "God isn't really there. He isn't there to help me when they beat me and he isn't there to kill me when I do wrong – So either he is there and he doesn't really care about me, or he isn't there at all." The ever growing battle for my mind has just reached a new level of complexity. "Should I attempt to do good and fail or give in to the bad and be condemned?" I chose the latter. It was too hard to try to be good, and why try if God doesn't care anyway?

My older brother was always good. The stereotypical good son and bad son situation just like Cain and Abel. He seemed to have an impeccable conscience that kept him always doing right. It didn't seem fair. Why was it so easy for him? But he still got his fair share of beatings – good son or not. Dad's temper was not reserved for just wrongdoing. It could strike out at even the best person over the smallest of infractions. It makes me shudder when I think about some of the beatings that I watched my brothers take.

This night of waiting was unusually long. The thoughts about good versus evil and God's failure to help kept me company. My mind seemed to be my only friend and companion to talk me through everything. Nobody else cared. I was all alone. I was captain and king of the uninhabited Island of Me. Maybe the only person to save me would have to be myself. I visualized turning myself into a king. King Brian the Lion racing into battle and victoriously tearing all those who hurt him into shreds.

As I sat in silence and waited, I began to wonder what I could do or say to lessen the punishment. To say or do something that would cause dad to somehow show pity and mercy to me and forego the, what now seemed inevitable execution of my hind quarters and anything else that should happen to get in the way.

My mind raced furiously to come up with a plan. What about, "I was just joking, or I was temporarily insane." The plea of temporary insanity never worked well with dad. He was really big on taking personal responsibility for your actions. "That's it!" I thought almost out loud. "Personal responsibility is my ticket out of this mess." My mind worked fast to recall a lecture earlier in the month from one of my Bible teachers at school. The guilt trip seemed to work so well for him that I decided it was time to turn the tables and give dad a dose of his own medicine. The lecture, as I recalled, was about a father whose son had done something wrong. When the father confronted the son about his misdeed, the son said "But I saw you do it last week so I thought it was ok for me to do it." The father was instantly shamed by what the son had said and saw how his son watched and learned from his every move. He then took personal responsibility and apologized to his son for setting a bad example and vowed to be a better father and role model for him to learn from.

Could it really work? Well it was surely worth a shot. Dad would walk in and I would tell him I learned it all from him. And then dad would see how I looked up to him and tried to learn from him, just like the boy in the story. And then dad would dedicate his life to being a better father and our relationship as father and son would grow and blossom into a loving and healthy relationship. And then dad would love me and hug me tightly and we would live happily ever after. This was going to be a great day – A day that would change a relationship forever.

So with strategy in hand I wait – and wait – and wait. It is now past 10pm and I am still waiting. Dad was extra late tonight but this was nothing out of the ordinary. He was the pastor and people needed his help and so he helped. I couldn't help but feel that he cared more about them and their problems than he did about me. "Does anyone really care about me" I wondered as another belief slowly begins to form in my fragile psyche – No one really cares about me but me, so maybe I should look out for me.

As the time approached 10:15 I decided on a new strategy for dealing with dad. "Why not pretend I'm asleep?" It was brilliant. I hurriedly ran to the dresser and grabbed my pajamas. I shed the blue jeans and 3 extra pairs of underwear that I had put on earlier as extra padding, quickly threw on my pajamas, turned off the light and jumped up into my bed on the top row of my custom made bunk bed. I thought this would work for sure. Dad would be tired and I would be acting as if I was asleep. Surely dad wouldn't want to wake me up.

At 10:31pm my ears suddenly raise as they perk up with anticipation at the sound of a car coming down the lonely gravel road toward the house. I listened intently to see if the car would pass by or stop and turn in. The noise stopped and then was followed by the slamming of the car door. This was it. My heart began to race almost as fast as my mind. I heard the front door open and then slam quickly shut. It sounded like an angry slam of the door. Was it angry?

I had now been waiting in my room for over 6 hours. I closed my eyes tightly and wondered if my well-engineered plan would work out properly. I listened intently to each ominous footstep as dad's feet heavily walked across the dining room and into the living room where mom and my three brothers sat watching TV. Everyone was still awake well past their bedtimes. Because we all slept in the same room on 2 sets of bunk beds that dad and grandpa had made, no one was allowed to enter the room until my fate had been decided and the punishment carried out.

I listened to the muffled voices through the wall as I tried to make out what they were saying. It sounded like Mom was explaining the infraction in detail and then appeared to give her 2 cents as to what the punishment should entail. And then it was quiet. I strained to listen for any sign of what was happening. Part of me wanted to get it over with but still there was the piece of me that hoped the punishment could be averted.

And then with almost no warning the door flew open. It came open so fast that I was startled and immediately flinched. My body jerked forward and my eyes opened and locked directly on the eyes of my father as if looking at a mugger or would be attacker about to pounce on its prey. Dad glared at me as he noticed the fear in my eyes. He fed off of the fear and seemed to enjoy watching us boys squirm under his thumb of tyranny and fear. He demanded fear and respect above all else. Any act of the children was seen as defining who he was and how it made him look to other people. Acts not deemed appropriate were direct disrespect and treated harshly.

Any attempt to act asleep was now gone. Plan b was now in full effect and my extra padding was not on my body! As dad slowly approached I tried to mentally prepare all of the words I intended to say. As I fidgeted beneath the covers of my bed, and dad took each step closer and closer to me, I considered scrapping plan b and just pleading guilty to the charges at hand. Each step seemed to take hours as my mind made hundreds of calculations and decisions per step. With each step my mind changed as to whether I should use plan b or not. And then we were face to face, fear still showing strongly in my tiny eyes.

"Your mom said you mouthed off to your brother" dad said very matter of fact like.
"Yes sir" I meekly responded.
"What did you say?"
"I told him to leave me alone and that he could play when I was finished."
"Why did you say that?"
It was almost like a set up I thought. Like a softball pitched in nice and slow right across the low outside corner of the plate. I paused as I contemplated my use of plan b until my mouth opened and it just came out. My mouth seemed to be my greatest enemy second only to my mind. It routinely blurted out whatever it felt like saying only to be followed up seconds later by a thought from the mind that said "Did you really just say that out loud." Dad would always say "Brian, don't let your mouth write checks your butt can't cover." And this time was no different. My mouth was writing one of the biggest checks it had ever written and there was not nearly enough collateral to cover what was about to happen.

"Why did you say that?" dad repeated as I continued to pause. "Well, I heard you say it once so I thought it was ok for me to say it." The reaction was almost instantaneous; faster than I even expected. I was ready for dad to go into a deep thought process of how he was wrong and then apologize; just like in the story. But I knew right away that was not going to happen. I could see the anger welling up in dad's eyes. I was very good at reading people's reactions. From a young age I learned to know when to quickly back out of a dangerous situation and run for cover. I found it best to stay under cover and out of harms way when I saw trouble in their eyes.

In a split second it all began. Dad's hand flew forward and grabbed me by the arm and pulled me swiftly out of the top bunk of the bed and threw me onto the floor. I landed on my side and started to roll quickly around to catch my bearings and see which way was up and from where the next blow might be coming from. But before I could see it coming a powerful foot from dads left leg caught me mid torso and just below the arm pit. I slid across the floor and into the wall as I gained my position and sat up with arms raised trying desperately to defend whatever was coming next. It was all happening so fast. "I'm the dad!" he screamed at the top of his lungs. "I get to do what I want to do and you do what I tell you to!" He hung directly over me and screamed down on top of me as I cowered in fear. "Go get me the paddle!" he yelled as mom left from watching in the doorway to do his bidding.

I had heard dad preach in church many times about spanking. He was a big proponent of corporal punishment. "Spare the rod and spoil the child is my motto" he would cheerfully spout to all those with unruly children. He taught that parents should never spank in anger. That if they were angry they should have a cool down period before disciplining their child. I marveled at the hypocrisy of moments like this. To hear him teach in public one thing and do the exact opposite in private only seemed to embolden me to do the same. I began to live life with my own motto of "I can do whatever I want as long as I don't get caught."

It wasn't long until mom showed up with the paddle. Now dad took a lot of pride in his paddles. He made them himself from solid oak milled to three quarters of an inch thick. Sometimes he would make you watch as he made a new paddle just so he could use it on you. The band saw would fire up with a high pitched sound of screaming steel slicing through wood at unimaginable speeds. The sound was unbearable knowing what would be the end use of an otherwise beautiful piece of wood. The router and sander would come next as it attempted to soften the edges of the handle so as not to wound the hands of the man applying the punishment. It would be a shame to get a splinter while beating someone with a piece of wood.

Dad continued to yell as he waited for the delivery of the paddle "I'm the dad! I get to do what I want and say what I want! You don't get to question me! I'm the dad!" Mom handed dad the paddle with a look of satisfaction that I was getting what I deserved for my act of defiance to authority.   Dad grabbed the paddle and hit me across the side of the leg as I lay on the ground and said "Get up and bend over the edge of the bed." Dad's fury was felt as he swung over and over and again and again. I screamed in pain and begged him to stop as I shrieked over and over "I'm sorry I was bad – I'll never do it again. I'm so sorry I was bad – I'll never do it again."

I rolled back in forth in cries of pain awaiting the last swing but it didn't seem to come. I moved back and forth on the bed always trying to have the paddle land in a different place on my body in an effort to give the pain in another place a chance to subside before receiving another violent strike. And then I heard the crack that I longed to hear as the paddle splintered into 3 different pieces. Three quarters of an inch of solid oak now lay in ruins. It was over... or so I thought. I was exhausted from screaming, crying and begging for my life and physically drained by the pain which permeated my whole body. But dad's rage was not finished. "I'm the dad. I get to do what I want to do and you have to do what I say" was still on his lips. With only the handle of his weapon left in his hand he threw it hitting me in the middle of my lower back as he began to take off his belt.

I was at a loss for thoughts. "What could I possibly have said or done that could have enraged him this badly? Or do they hate me this much? Am I so difficult to love? Will they ever love me?"

The belt was different as it sought to discover new areas that had not been attacked as of yet. The sides of the legs and the arms had yet to experience any welts and dad seemed determined to make sure I was covered from head to toe. Urine began to run down my legs soaking my pajama bottoms and the floor as my bladder gave way to the pain and the exhaustion of the beating. I hoped that dad would not notice.

My screaming subsided as dad began to tire. His heavy breathing was evident as he began to wind down from his rage induced overexertion. I laid face down on the bed still softly saying over and over "I'm sorry I was bad – I'll never do it again." But as usual dad had to close with one last sentiment "I'm the dad. I get to do what I want. You will respect me and don't you ever tell me what to do again." His back slowly turned and he walked out without another word.

I still lay face down on the bed. I wondered if it was actually over or if the door would swing back open only to continue the melee with yet another weapon. My pain was beyond anything I had ever felt before. Pain shot back and forth in waves across my entire body while cruelly pausing in random locations to make sure no one place was left out. My finger throbbed in agony. I glanced down at my swollen knuckle and was pretty sure my finger was broken as it began to swell to twice its size. It had forgotten its place and strayed into the path of the paddle. The bruises and welts were too numerous to count and they stung deeply with the hurt of disdain and abandonment. In this state of total brokenness I longed for someone to hold me and nurse my wounds. Someone to tell me that I was alright and that everything would be ok. But no one came. And no one would be coming. I was all alone.

Chapter 12
Revelation
Step 1 – It Will Work... Until it Doesn't

Now that we have identified some of our methods of control we can ask ourselves another thought provoking question. Why do I even need surrender? Things hurt here and there and I wish certain aspects of my life were better but I really like most of my life and I just don't want to let it all go. Maybe it's a relationship that you know is wrong or an addiction that you don't think is really hurting anyone. What is it that you feel guilty about that keeps you up at night and robs your waking hours of peace? Whatever that thing is, it must come to the point where you are ready to put it on the table for discussion if you would like to find peace. Once it is on the table we have to scrub it through the filter of true guilt versus false guilt. True guilt comes from God and false guilt comes from the deceiver. Is what you are feeling about this issue condemnation from the deceiver or is it compelling love from Christ trying to lead you to a better life. It is important to be open to the idea that maybe there is a plan and a purpose for my life and that just maybe, it was designed by a God who loves me and wishes the best for me. Many people will embark on this journey and never finish because they don't trust or believe that God has their best interest in mind. If you are harboring hurt, mistrust and anger towards God we will deal with that in a later chapter. For now, just be open to the idea that what you know and believe about God may not be correct and that a completely different concept of who God is could exist.

My journey started out just like this. I was angry with God and didn't believe that I could trust Him. But then I came to realize that many of my beliefs about God were built out of someone else's desire to control me. What I believed was founded in what they had told me and thus was tainted by their personal bent on life. In short, what I believed as truth was not my own. It was given to me by someone else. I only believed it all because of my trust in the person conveying it all to me and because the current circumstances seemed to support them. But there comes a point when we all need to grow up and define our own reality. Whether what we were taught as children was truth, a lie or a very confusing mixture of the two, we must reach the point where we search out the truth for ourselves. We can no longer rely on our parent's church and our upbringing for all of our beliefs. For me, it was upon this realization that I decided to throw out everything I had learned as a child and learn for myself. Of course reading takes time and effort but I had a desire to know the truth.

This was the point where I believe that I activated a key promise from God to anyone who is willing to activate it. This promise is beautiful and dear to my heart as it changed my life forever. His promise – Ask and you will receive, seek and you will find, knock and the door will be opened. Many people may look at this and take it at face value by asking for a new car or a new job and then demanding that God give it because, well because you said all I had to do was ask. But what if the application is much different? What if He is talking about Himself? Ask for Me and you will receive Me. Seek Me and you will find Me. Knock on My door and I will open it to you.

Maybe at some point you have asked God for something more in your life. Maybe you asked Him to show you who He is.

Once the promise is activated the refining process begins. In this process God has to remove from us who we think we are in order to replace it with who he created us to be. This process can be as painful as the peeling off of our flesh. Once it begins we look around and say, "Whoa, wait a minute God. This isn't what I asked for. I asked for peace. I asked for you to "bless" me. I asked for you to make everything better, not worse."

But this is where we should push forward. We push forward because there is a battle going on for our heart, mind and soul. What if there is a God that really does love us and want us to live a life filled with love and peace? What if there is an alternate force inside each of us that wants to subvert and derail that peace and happiness? What if its main job is to make us believe a lie about who we think we are?

In the writings of Apostle Paul we hear him discuss a force such as this which he calls the flesh. He says that living in the flesh will work for us for a while because it really can feel good to live a lie. It feels good that is until it finally stops working. The book of Hebrews mentions that there is pleasure in sin but only for a season. It will be fun until it's not fun anymore. How many people reach the end of that rope and end up tying a noose and hanging themselves by it? How many people looked like they were happy and had everything only to see them destitute, strung out in despair, or even dead.

So what are the indications that living a life based on a lie is no longer working? There is that nagging feeling of restlessness or the feeling that something just isn't right. Even when things are going well, I just can't quite connect with my life or the lives of those around me. There must be something missing or something more to life. One of the major indicators that it isn't working anymore is the pain caused by the consequences of our choices. One of my favorite quotes is "I hold you personally responsible for the choices I make that ruin my life." It seems so much easier to consistently blame everything on someone else, our station in life, our upbringing, or on that horrible event that happened. But Brian, if only I had been born on the other side of town or had better parents or gotten that job or married the right guy my life would be better. Personal responsibility is not a very popular topic in today's culture. Maybe it's time to take personal responsibility for your life. Maybe it's time to evaluate all of the excuses you make for why you are in the stage of life you are in.

Unfortunately, pain is the predecessor to true life change. Have you ever heard of someone without any problems in their life waking up in the morning and saying, you know what, I think I'll change my life today. As mentioned earlier, until the pain of remaining the same exceeds the pain of change, we will not choose to change. But at this point I really don't want us to focus on the change. I want us to focus on the surrender. So that changes our statement a little. Until the pain of remaining the same exceeds the pain of surrender then we will not surrender.

This leads us to what we've all been waiting for – Step 1 on the path to surrender. Step one – We must experience pain or discomfort in remaining the same. You have to reach the point where you don't like where you are in life enough to make a change. And not necessarily a change in our actions but a change in the way we think. A change in what we do may only be maintained for a time as a habit. A change in how we think has the capacity to change a life forever because a change in thinking will eventually change what we do.

C.S. Lewis said that "We are half-hearted creatures, fooling about with drink and sex and ambition when infinite joy is offered us, like an ignorant child who wants to go on making mud pies in a slum because he cannot imagine what is meant by the offer of a holiday at the sea. We are far too easily pleased." Try and let that sink in a little bit. We are settling for just 'good enough' and we think that it's a steak dinner when it is actually a mud pie in the slum compared to what God has planned for us if we would only let Him take us there. The kicker is that we can't go there while we are trying to hold on to the control in our lives.

What if you actually believed that what you currently experience that you think you can't let go of is just a mud pie in the slum? What if you actually believed that a gracious and loving God wants you to experience infinite, unexplainable joy and peace in your life? Chances are that if you accepted both of these beliefs you would be compelled to give up what you are holding on to so tightly and embark on an adventure to find a new perspective for your life. A new perspective filled with freedom from the past, hope for the future and inexplicable peace and joy in the present.

I mention a new perspective because we are currently in bondage to the systems of control that exist in the world. We wear the chains of social and religious rules and regulations and subscribe to the fact that we cannot step outside of them for fear of being an outsider. Well this is my invitation for you to unplug yourself from "the mud pie in the slum" and begin the journey to find your "holiday at sea."

One of the most brilliant tricks the devil ever devised was to offer different branches of organized religion to the world. He has kept us all fighting since the beginning of time over doctrine and standards instead of looking at Christ and what he did for us. Religion is the wool that has been pulled over our eyes so that we cannot see the Truth. We fight to the death over our faith and are not responsible for the victims that lay in our path because we are totally and completely justified. Do you think the Christians that started the Crusades were justified? Of course they felt they were. How about Hitler or the Salem witch trials? Both justified by religion.

Are all of the religious standards and convictions important to God anyway? When Christ was asked "What is the most important law that we can live to uphold", He only gave us two. Make sure you get baptized and make sure you tell all your friends that what they're doing is wrong. No, of course he didn't say that.

He said "Love the Lord your God with all your heart mind and soul and love your neighbor as yourself." He felt that these two things were enough. He felt that these two things would lead to everything else. You see if we love God with everything we have than we love him more then we love ourselves. We then give preference to what He wants for us and let go of what we think we want. This is true surrender. When we let go of everything we are holding on to and are free to receive that love back from God we are fulfilled as we experience Love, Acceptance, Worth and Security. When we embrace His love we are then able to share it with those around us freely and without any expectations.

Is it your time? I believe it is. This is your time to unplug from the system to which you have been bound and look for a new way of thinking – a free way of thinking that leads to peace in your heart, mind and soul. Let's review the journaling for this week that will set us up to be ready for step 2.

1. In what areas of my life am I feeling pressure?
2. In what areas of my life do I always have to be in control?
3. What other people in my life do I attempt to control?

Chapter 13
Redemption
Decision Affects Destiny

I did not sleep well that night. I tossed and turned and frequently jumped up out of bed as my dreams betrayed me by playing the incident over and over. Like a bad rerun of Tom and Jerry. But this was no cartoon. The bumps, bruises, and welts were real. A fact of which I was reminded each time I rolled over in my sleep.

The next morning as I dressed for school I was numb with pain. My senses seemed dull and my mind in a fog. I dressed myself without thinking and then sat and wondered if anything was ever going to be different. Did I have to endure this for the rest of my life? Life – was this life? Was it always going to be this way? With these heavy thoughts on my mind I headed to the kitchen for breakfast. Maybe food would help take my mind off of my plight.

When I reached the kitchen mom instantly looked at me with a look of disapproval. "What are you trying to pull mister" she barked emphatically. I looked at her stunned and disillusioned as if to say "What did I do this time?" "You want your friends to see, don't you? Do you want to get your father into trouble?" I looked at her, dazed and confused, my mind trying to quickly assess the situation to see what I had done and how much trouble I was in. I was very fragile and broken and didn't know how much more I could take. She reached down and grabbed my arm. I winced in pain as she grabbed directly onto one of my many bruises.

As I looked down at my arms I noticed the total carnage. My arms were covered in black and blue welts and I was wearing a short sleeved shirt. The belt had done its job well. "Are you trying to get your father in trouble?" she repeated. I was too tired to think and just stood there staring back at her. My mind was numb and completely exhausted. My body no longer shook with fear as it seemed to have accepted its fate – its fate as an object of pain to be pummeled with anything within reaching distance.

I was glad that dad was gone early this morning. At least she couldn't call on him to go another few rounds with me. "What's going through your mind?" she asked repugnantly. "How dare you talk to your father like that – What were you thinking?" I assumed she was talking about my attempt to shame dad the night before. "Such disrespect will not be tolerated." I had no response other than the cold indifferent stare glaring back at her. "You need to learn respect and where your place is young man."

Knowing the paddle was broken and dad's belt gone made me feel a little safer. Most of the other weapons in the house didn't hurt as bad as those two did. And so mom reached for the kitchen drawer and grabbed the old standby – the always quick and easy to grab wooden spoon. I assumed the position by leaning forward and grasping the counter in front of me.

The spoon tried to awaken last night's bruises and welts but was unsuccessful. It hurt but at the same time almost felt good. The pain slowly turned from mere discomfort into food, sustenance, and fuel for my anger. With each swat the indifference on my face and in my heart grew as if throwing gasoline on a brush fire. But the indifference and rage would again turn to numbness. And the cold feeling of being completely alone would walk with me throughout the entire day. "Go to your room, put on a long sleeve shirt, and get in the car. We're leaving for school." I did as I was told. What else was there to do?

I didn't hear much from my teachers in class that day. My face was sullen and pale. My eyes looked straight ahead as if looking beyond everything in sight and into another dimension. Each step was wrought with screeching pain as my pants rubbed caustically against my wounds. Even the act of sitting at my desk had been reduced to pure torture. I peered outside at the icy blanket of snow and longed to go lay prostrate in its cold grip to cool the burning of my skin.

Several people saw the deadened look in my eyes and even asked me if I was ok. Is it possible that someone does care? I wanted to burst into tears and rip off my clothes to show everyone the masterpiece of pain that covered my body. But it wouldn't help. Dad was the boss. He always won. I had seen him put many a person in their place. And their place was always cowering in fear beneath his thumb. Was there anyone to help? "I'm all alone – It's just me – No one is coming to save me."

The phrase repeats in my head as I sit at my crossroads. "No one is coming to save me", I think as my teeth begin to chatter ever so slightly. I sit at the pinnacle of desperation looking to make a decision that will affect my destiny. One decision will lead to death and another can lead to life. The decision for life can again be broken down further into types of life that will be lived based on decisions made in this moment. I have a choice to live a life of hatred, rage and anger – a choice to live a life of indifference – a choice to exact a lifetime of revenge – a choice to completely forget everything and try to live a normal life – or a combination of several or all of the choices put together. The choice I always heard in church was forgiveness. But forgiveness was the furthest thing from my mind right now. I would never forgive them. How could I? It was an unthinkable option to be blocked completely from thought or mention in my clouded mind.

With every situation we face in life there are options. One

option seems to be the easy, wide road option, and the other is the hard, narrow path option. It would definitely be so much easier to end it all and stop the pain right now, but what are the choices? What if there is a choice that can change the course of generations of hurt, pain, and abuse.

Every one of us will at some point in our life come to a place that demands more of us than we are prepared to give. To ask us to step up to the plate and make a decision that will shape the course of our future, the future of our family and children, and the lives of everyone around us.

My belief system and ultimately my life, was shaped by two things. First of all, it was shaped by the influences of people in authority such as my parents and teachers. As much as people in these positions may not like it, they have the effect of influencing those in their path. Secondly, it was shaped by the experiences I went through on a daily basis. While both are very capable of shaping a person, the second will always trump the first when put head to head. The influence of people will continue to be our center and hold us in check until an experience takes place that contradicts what we are being told. I heard dad say it often, "Your walk talks louder than your talk talks." I understood this but didn't feel dad knew what he was saying. Dad also always said "Do what I say, not what I do." Talk about a contradiction.

As a child I was told that the stove was hot and I was not to touch it. I believed this because I was told by someone I trusted that it was hot. One day I accidentally touched the stove and burnt my hand. I then was enlightened with an entirely new understanding and appreciation, through my experience, that the stove is actually hot. I had felt the pain of the heat and definitely did not plan on touching it again. Our experiences in life are the strongest factors in determining who we become.

My experiences and how I felt about them gave me a laundry list of beliefs about myself and my place in the world. As I sit perched atop the ultimate decision for my destiny, my beliefs dance slowly through my mind one at a time as if taunting me and daring me to do the unthinkable.

"I am all alone"

"I am a bad boy"

"I am a bad person"

"Nobody loves me"

"I am unlovable"

"Everybody hates me"

"I am despised and detestable"

"My life doesn't matter"

"I am worthless"

The 'I am' lies were the most dangerous. They went deep into my core and controlled my belief in who I was and in some sick way seemed to predict my future. I once was good – I thought. But now I might as well be what I am – Alone, Bad, and Unlovable.

And now using this false information I am about to make a very important decision. It is easy to see how a life can be so easily altered by its own internal thought process. Each belief can become a self-fulfilling prophecy as it carries "I am worthless" through to its logical end result – death.

Some people are brought to this point at a young age when it seems totally unfair that a person so young is asked to make such a decision. A choice between death and changing the way of life for future generations seems to be a lot of pressure to put on a 10 year old. But not many of us actually get to choose who our parents are, in what type of home we will grow up, and what events and circumstances we will encounter at any moment.

I slowly stood up from my crouched position and stared down over the edge at the crisp snow down below. I was now trembling from the cold and wondered if the unsteadiness might cause me to slip and fall. The fear of what it might feel like to hit the ground and not die gripped at my mind and would not let go. Let's face it – my luck so far in life hadn't been that great. If it continued in the same manner I would end up living through the jump and get beat on top of that for trying something so stupid.

As the coldness ran to my core it seemed to awaken the dark cold indifference I had begun to feel during the morning's wooden spoon beating. But now the strength and intensity was much greater. My indifference fanned the coals of anger that lay deep in my soul and again the flame was lit and began to burn out of control. I began to feel warm as the hot blood of rage surged through my veins pumping faster and faster with every beat of my heart. "No one is ever going to hurt me again" I thought as I stood tall and proud.

A smile crossed my face almost like a grimace as I felt the pride of taking control of my life back. "It will be over soon and no one will ever hurt me again. I am in control of my life. I can take care of myself and I don't need anybody else." My will grew stronger with each repeat of the belief in my mind. "I am in control of my life. I have to take care of myself. No one will ever hurt me again."

I raised my fist to the sky and repeated my new mantra. "I don't need anybody else. It's just me and I have to take care of me." My fist shook angrily at God, the universe, or maybe just at life. I wasn't really sure who to be angry at. But if God was out there he sure wasn't breaking down any doors to come save me.

I felt a renewed sense of power in my new beliefs. I slowly backed away from the edge as my mind worked to put into place the groundwork and foundation of its new plan – a plan that was needed to survive – a plan to detach mentally and emotionally from everyone and everything – to ball up tightly as if under attack and protect the core and vital organs – to build an impenetrable fortress of walls around my feelings, my heart and my soul.

This wall would be built with the strongest materials available. The bricks were mixed out of sadness, disappointment, and hurt. They were then formed in a mold of indifference, fired in a furnace of rage, and cooled by the coldness of my heart. The wall must be made to last so the best and strongest mortar must be used. The mortar was a mixture of sadness from all of my dreams, goals, and aspirations lost and left behind. This was an impenetrable wall. The best wall pain and suffering could build.

Every dream I ever had about who I was or what I wanted to do as a child would be locked within these walls. Dreams were not important anymore. Protection was all that mattered so my mind began working on its defenses. A wall without defenses is vulnerable so I had to keep building.

Turrets were placed strategically at every point from which I could imagine there might be an attack. Each turret was armed with a barrage of auto firing arrows and shields. The shields were skillful at deflection and blame shifting but the arrows were the most dangerous of my weapons. My arrows could see through anyone's armor and search for their most vulnerable spot. Once it saw where they could be hurt the most the arrow could skillfully and quickly fire itself and sink deeply into anyone who approached my castle.

This was a castle of isolation from everything that hurt. But there was a flaw in the castles construction. The castle was built with such haste that no doors were added. The walls were constructed with me inside – no way in – and no way out. No feeling or pain was allowed to enter – and no happiness or joy was allowed to leave. I had heard the saying that no man is an island but I was sure that wasn't true. I was convinced that I was an island and had now built everything I needed to take care of myself. "I am all alone. It's just me. I have to take care of myself."

As my mind worked furiously on my new defense systems, my feet were ever so slowly shuffling backward away from the edge. A feeling of power and that I was in control of my life and my destiny swept over me. My will to live had narrowly won the battle with its decision to fortify and defend. I crept slowly back across the roof and into the attic window. As I suspected, no one had even noticed I had been gone for so long. And try as they did, no one could hurt me anymore. I was locked safely behind my walls in my Castle of Indifference.

Your homework for this week is to identify the walls that exist in your life. When were they built and why did you build them? Be as detailed as you possibly can because the end goal is the dismantling of these walls. You will need to remember everything you can about your walls purpose so that when the time is right each wall can be taken down piece by piece.

Chapter 14
Revelation
Step 2 – It Hurts and I Can't Fix It

Step 1 left us with the idea that we want to make the decision to challenge the norms in our lives and choose to embark on a journey of self-discovery. Step 2 brings us to a realization about the capacity that we believe we have within us to do everything ourselves. This step brings us face to face with the fact that "my life hurts and I can't fix it." Now this is a really hard pill to swallow. Especially if you are used to fixing everything for everyone around you at all times. It's kind of like watching someone try to put one of those little tiny screws into the back of a small game watching them fumble around with it makes every fiber of your being want to jump in and scream "Let me do it!" We have an overwhelming desire to want to maintain control and do it ourselves.

So why is it that we can't do it ourselves? It is because in our power we are only able to affect change on our habits for a time. We can focus on a behavior and decide to work on it but we are not able to go directly to the source and make it completely go away. Why is it that some alcoholics stop cold turkey and never desire to drink another drop and others never stop fighting the urge to grab a bottle? Could it be because one is fighting the battle himself and the other knows that the battle has already been fought and won?

So what battle am I referring to? Let's take a look at the book of Jeremiah to try to get another perspective on how we see this process. Jeremiah wrote in chapter 17 that *"The heart is hopelessly dark and deceitful, a puzzle that no one can figure out. But I, God, search the heart and examine the mind. I get to the heart of the human. I get to the root of things. I treat them as they really are, not as they pretend to be."*

What Jeremiah is really saying here is that it can be difficult to see who we really are. We can be so sure of who we think we are that we will fight tooth and nail to make sure our point of view is seen and heard. But God tells us in Jeremiah that our heart is a puzzle that we can't figure out and that only He is able to truly search our heart and examine our mind. Only He can lead us to the truth of who we really are and reveal to us the lie of what or who we are pretending to be.

As we go through our day we tend to wear different masks as we enter different settings and social situations. Let's call these masks that we wear identities. We each have an overall identity of who we believe we are and we project it to others so that they will see us the way we want to be seen. Let me give you an example. If I am in a meeting at the office I may want to be seen as an aggressive hard worker so that is the mask that I will wear. If I am going into a meeting with my daughter's teacher I may want to appear more passive so I won't be called on to help with the PTA. The problem comes when we begin to believe the performance of the mask that we are wearing and we become what we are projecting. This problem is further exacerbated by the fact that we forget that we ever even put on the mask. Step 2 is about asking God to do what He said He would do in Jeremiah. We do this by asking Him to search our heart and examine our minds to make us aware of any lies we are projecting and reveal to us the truth of who he created us to be – to reveal to us our true identity.

Once we ask God to step in and help we can now take a look at the masks we are wearing and start the process of removing them a little at a time. We can do this by asking a simple question in our journal and spending some time applying a question to our lives. What have I been fighting for? When I wake up what is my sole purpose for everything I do? If you let it sink in you will notice that the answer is identity. We are fighting to make sure that everyone else notices us and knows who we are and the contribution that we make to society. Have you ever noticed that when someone tells a story that invariably everyone else is reminded of a story that involves themselves and then each person in turn tells the story of 'me'.

Throughout each day I am fighting for the right to be heard, for my wants, needs and desires to be fulfilled, and for everything that I feel I am entitled to, to come my way. This fight for most begins at a very young age and will last for the rest of our lives or until we realize that life is about something bigger than we are.

When we attempt to accomplish this on our own we start out with the best intentions but never quite get to where we want to go. Paul had plenty to say about this process in Romans chapter 7.

For if I know the law but still can't keep it, and if the power of sin within me keeps sabotaging my best intentions, I obviously need help!

Paul realized that he knew all the right religious answers but that the power of sin constantly came in to sabotage his best intentions.

I realize that I don't have what it takes. I can will it, but I can't do it. I decide to do good, but I don't really do it; I decide not to do bad, but then I do it anyway.

Next he shows us that it doesn't really matter how much he

believed in his ability to change himself. He is saying here that he can will himself to do good, decide he wants to do better and even decide that he isn't going to do wrong, but then he ends up doing wrong anyway.

I truly delight in God's commands, but it's pretty obvious that not all of me joins in that delight. Parts of me covertly rebel, and just when I least expect it, they take charge. I've tried everything and nothing helps. I'm at the end of my rope.

We could make the argument that Paul had more enlightenment about Christ than anyone else ever but even he knew that there was a problem. He said that he delighted in what God wanted but he knew that something else in him was going to come in and try to take charge. I've tried everything and nothing works. Now this is the point where many of us give up. We are fed up with trying to live the way we think is right, or do what we think we are supposed to do, and we just don't want another failure on our record so we just quit trying. But Paul didn't finish there.

Is there no one who can do anything for me? Isn't that the real question? The answer, thank God, is that Jesus Christ can and does.

He finishes by saying that Jesus Christ is the answer to this problem. He is clearly telling us that we cannot do this process on our own. As much as we want to take hold of the reigns and say "let me do it", we have to give Him permission to do the work that He wants to do in our lives. It may be giving Him permission to let you feel what He wants you to feel even though your feelings have been locked up for most of your life. It doesn't matter what it is. We just have to know that we can't do it on our own. We must ask Him to do it for us and remain open and willing to what He has for us as He does His work in us.

This leads us back to the problem of identity. How do I make sure that my identity is always open enough to be challenged? We can do this by adopting an attitude of having a flexible identity. If we are only the sum of our past experiences then our identity has the capacity to change if we introduce new experiences. Who I think I am is only my current interpretation of who I think I am based on the experiences so far in my life.

Let me give you an illustration. When automobiles where introduced scientists agreed that if a human body were to exceed 25 miles per hour its insides would explode. They strongly discouraged anyone from attempting to create a faster car and even had certain inventors arrested for trying to create a faster car. This belief was based on the information at hand and the past experience of the scientists involved. Once new information and experience was introduced they could and did change their opinions. The problem came with the fact that they were so convinced that they were right. Once the 25 mph barrier was broken they raised the speed to a higher number and were once again adamant. Of course we now have a land speed record of over 450 mph and an air speed record of over 2000 mph.

Because our identity is affected by experiences we must also be aware of how negative experiences shape who we are. Every event follows a logical progression along the path to changing who we think we are. When an event happens we immediately have a feeling. That feeling can lead to a belief and the belief will usually lead to the implementation of a coping mechanism to help us deal with what happened.

Let's take a look at a young girl in second grade. The teacher asks a question and she raises her hand to answer. The teacher ridicules the answer in front of the entire class – Event. The young girl instantly becomes flush with embarrassment and feels confused, belittled and stupid – Feeling. This feeling leads her to believe "I am not as smart as everyone else. I am stupid. I don't know how to speak in front of other people." – Beliefs. These beliefs lead her to the most dangerous part. "I will never raise my hand again" – Coping Mechanism. Something has been added to her identity that changed who she thinks she is. She may have something valuable to add to the meeting she is in at work, but she can't raise her hand.

As you read the stories of my childhood you can see the beliefs and coping mechanisms that were born through neglect or necessity and how they controlled my life for many years. I had to reach the point where I raised the white flag for my broken identity. I had to finally come to terms with the fact that I had lost the fight for who I thought I was and I wanted and needed some help with revealing my true identity and who I was created to be.

Probably the hardest part of letting go of who you think you are is the fear of not knowing who you will be on the other side of that transition. Tearing out all of the pages that have been written in the book of who I think I am and staring at a blank page that has not been written yet is very overwhelming. The best tool that we have to manage this change is to let go of who we think we are and choose to believe that God will come through on His promise to reveal to us the identity that He created in us from the beginning of time. And the best news is that we don't have to strive to do all of the work. We only need to step out of the way and give Him control to do His work in us in His time.

Your homework for this chapter will be to write down three or more areas of your life where you have experienced brokenness either in the past or are currently feeling brokenness in the present. Be specific with your stories and give them to God believing that no matter how hard or how heavy they are, He can handle it. He wants you to let Him walk with you in your story because it is not only your story – It is His story. He has been with you every step of the way. One of my favorite lines from any movie is from The Count of Monte Cristo. The priest tells Edmund Dantes that God will use him for good. Edmund confesses that he does not believe in God due to his anger that God did not come rescue him as he was falsely imprisoned and beaten mercilessly.

The priest responds "It does not matter that you do not believe in God. He believes in you." Whether we believe He is there or not does not matter. I do not have to believe in gravity for it to hold my feet to the ground. It is always there and always at work. Even if He is the one you are angry with, tell him in your journal.

Chapter 15
Redemption

Cold Blooded Killer

We often wonder what creates that unrepentant member of society that ruefully abandons all conscience and morals and proceeds through life with willful destruction of everything and everyone in their path. I was on my way to becoming that person. Nothing was beyond me. My conscience no longer existed which gave me license to do or try anything. Nothing seemed wrong anymore and guilt did not exist. If God thought what they did to me was ok then anything I could do to anyone else was fair game.

I looked for opportunities to pass on the pain that had so maliciously been given to me. The imparting of my own pain to anything around me seemed to somehow appease the screaming of my own demons. I started by hitting and throwing but escalated quickly to torture of anything that was in my path.

My favorite muse and tormentor was fire. Fire seemed to breathe and whisper as it moved in and around whatever it decided to consume. To me, the fire could talk. I heard its subtle beckoning to me and its desire to be released to feed. On several occasions I even allowed the fire to eat my own flesh. The pain was excruciatingly delightful. My pain threshold had to be 10 times that of a normal human. To me pain felt good and reminded me that I was alive – and made me believe that I was in total control.

My classmates received their own daily doses from my excess of pain. The once mischievous, playful eyes had grown dark and now only looked for places in which to land my arrows. I was quick witted with my barbs and tossed them skillfully at anyone who dared come near my fortress.

Dad and I didn't talk or see each other much. I did my best to steer clear of both mom and dad. Work with the farmer bailing hay kept me busy enough to only be seen at dinner time and that was the best way to keep it.

At age 14 we left the frigid, bone chilling cold of Michigan and headed south. Dad was offered a job as a pastor of a church down in Georgia. Dad always had trouble staying in one place for too long. It was like the place would start to crawl up under his skin and irritate him something fierce. I had already noticed the oddities going on with dad. I wasn't sure what was going on but I knew that something was not right.

I saw everything. They assumed I didn't. My defenses kept me quiet and in the shadows but I definitely saw through them like looking through glass. Years of practice at reading body language and facial expressions had made me an expert. I knew what was going to happen long before it transpired. I knew the secret. It was all in the eyes. You look at anybody's eyes long enough and they'll open their soul to you. The eyes tell you who is lying and who's telling the truth. Everyone around here was a liar to some degree or another. In this climate you had to lie to survive. You had to lie just to keep up. You had to lie just to keep from being eaten by the big dogs at the top of the food chain.

Dad wasn't the only one who needed a change. Mom's doctor said she would do better in a warmer climate. The climate was warmer and the pay more than double dad's current salary, so we loaded up the truck and headed for greener pastures. I was glad to trade in my northern accent for a soft slow southern drawl.

The Georgian accent was intoxicating. Not at all hick-like, it was distinguished and gentlemanly. It didn't take me long to start wearing it proudly. It grew on me like bumps on pickles - like it was just meant to be. And just forget about hearing the girls speak it. That was like the sound of angels speaking directly to God's ears. Georgia girls had truly been kissed by God with beauty and the voices of angels and I was anxious to get their attention.

The new school was rough on me at first. It's always tough trying to gain acceptance at a new school but I knew what to do. I had to mark my territory and fly my flag high and proud. My flag – was the flag from a town called Crazy. "That kid is freakin' nutz" was the reaction I went for and would usually go overboard to get.

I knew exactly what to do to gain acceptance in any situation. I was awkward and unsure of myself but definitely knew how to fake it. In church with a group of 'Jesus Junkies' I would tell my testimony and talk about all the souls I had saved from hell by getting them to pray 'the prayer'. In a group of girls I would smile coyly while slightly raising my left cheek and squinting my left eye as if I were the legendary John Wayne delivering the infamous "Well hello there little lady." And then after the delivery of my spectacular one liner, the girls would rub their hands across the top of my head and giggle with excitement. My head was usually buzzed short or spiked straight up. Either way it felt great to feel hands running softly across my head and was enjoyed immensely by all parties involved.

Now, while messing around with the 'Jesus Junkies' was fun and flirting with the girls even better, I loved my time with the guys. This was my chance to blow off steam and be who I was convinced I really was. No acting – no faking – just deep, dark, depraved indifference. To connect and be accepted with any group of guys I knew just what to do. As I approached the situation I would look for the worst possible thing that anyone could do. I looked for anything that could be done that would shock this crowd into a total uproar. My craziness had no boundaries and nothing was safe. I quickly identified two boys in my class who shared my rebellion for the establishment and we became inseparable.

The 3 amigos pillaged and plundered our way through a maze of hypocrisy as we attempted to walk the fine line between getting all you can out of life and not getting caught. The world was our oyster as we reached out to take it for all that it was while a church tried to teach us of a God who did not want us to have any of it. A God who demanded purity and perfection in exchange for His love or worse yet – He would punish us beyond anything we could ever imagine.

Dad used to tell the story of a young man in church that was punished for his misdeeds. It was his favorite story with which to spread fear, guilt, shame, and condemnation. The young man had gotten drunk the night before his wedding and slept with a prostitute. He never told his wife, who had thought they were both virgins, until they had their first child. Their little girl was born blind due to an STD he had picked up from the prostitute. When she was 4 years old she asked him why she couldn't see and all the other little girls could. He was so shamed by this question that he went into his bedroom and blew his brains out.

The moral of the story – Be good or God will smite your kids with a disease and drive you to kill yourself. Sounds like a wonderful God doesn't it? I always wondered if the story was actually true or if it was dreamed up or embellished to get all of the little church kids so scared that they would do what they were told. "No kissing or touching till your married" they always said. "God doesn't condone it" "What a crock of horse....." I thought. "If God is that mean do I really want him to be my God. Maybe there's a nicer one out there. Maybe there's one that likes me – or maybe even loves me a little."

But that was just wishful thinking. At this point I thought I had a really good handle on life. I believed that I was in control of my own destiny and that anything I wanted I had to create. I was pretty sure that if God was out there that He didn't want anything to do with me. I firmly believed that all He did was hurt people for not doing right.

Maybe if I was bad enough God just wouldn't worry about me at all. I no longer longed to be held nor wished to be touched by anyone. Touch was met by fear and distrust. I lived life on my terms and ignored the still ongoing ranting of an angry mother and the beatings from a deranged father. But I was comfortable with my interpretation of life. To me pain was part of existence and a necessity to make me strong. My dad had made me a strong man that could take anything you could dish out. You can't get this kind of toughness from just being pampered and sissified all the time. I was sure that I had life all figured out.

And then I met her. I was 16 and she was 14. Her eyes were soft and her smile was warm. Her cheeks were soft and subtle and surrounded by the loveliest locks of autumn brunette hair I had ever seen. Her eyes were the intoxicating color of aged Tennessee whiskey, a deep liquid pool of brown to get lost in for hours. She was petite and seemed almost tiny compared to me. She was the most beautiful thing I had ever seen. Her name – was Jennifer.

Chapter 16
Revelation
Step 3 – Decision and Desire

Step 1 heightened our awareness to the pain and discomfort of remaining in our current circumstances. Step 2 introduced the idea that we cannot fix the brokenness that exists in our lives. The next logical progression will be to make a decision to forgo what I have accepted as normal my entire life, tear out the pages that have already been written, and give God a clean slate to write on. Step 3 – Decide that you would like something different.

This step may sound too simple but I really want you to understand the psychology behind it and what happens mentally when we make a decision to head in a new direction.

When confronted with any decision we usually can view our choices as two different roads laid out in front of us. One of the roads is a 4 lane highway with rest stops and restaurants every two miles. This road is paved, completely level and there are lots of people on it for us to mingle with, get connected to, hook up with, and travel down the road together with. The other road is the road less traveled. When we look at it we can tell that the terrain is bumpy and there are many ups and downs. Just to look at it begs the obvious question of why would I even consider that road. Especially since all of those other people are taking the big, easy, beautiful, popular road. Some of my friends are on that road and if I take a different path then I may not get to see them as much or hang out any more.

The problem is that each road has a very different destination. The road that is wide leads to pain, sadness, ruin and destruction. Maybe not at first, the first 5, 10 or 15 years on this road may be a blast. Scripture tells us that there is pleasure in sin for a season. As we said in step 2, it will work until it stops working. Matthew chapter 7 lays this principle out clearly. *"For wide is the gate and broad is the road that leads to destruction, and many enter through it. But small is the gate and narrow the road that leads to life and only a few find it."*

The good news is that there is an alternative to the wide road. The truth is that the narrow road leads to Life. We can't see very far down the narrow road because trust is involved. If we knew all of the answers then faith wouldn't really be necessary. When we look at that small little road we have to trust and believe that something amazing is on that road that we don't want to miss out on. We won't be able to see around the first corner but we must believe that God has something for me on that narrow road and I want to be on it.

The next thing we want to do is write down our reasons for wanting to head down the narrow road. The most important part of making this decision is that you make the decision yourself. If someone else makes the decision for you then you are less likely to stay on the path. It's like an addict being dragged off to rehab and forced to stay. If it is not your decision to walk the narrow path in an effort to find something new and different then failure is most likely just around the corner.

Let's go ahead and do some homework. Pull out your journal and write 3 or more things that cause pain or a lack of peace in your life that you would like to change. These are the things that will motivate you and help you remember why you are on the narrow path. Every time you get to a difficult section of the path and you want to 'get off the ride' you will pull these reasons out to rekindle your desire for a new life. If you forget why you started your journey down this road then you are more likely to quit. Desire leads us to action. You must continually remind yourself what it was like to live in the past. We as humans tend to have a short memory and routinely fall back into pain that we just experienced a few months ago. It's kind of like going to eat at that really cheap pizza buffet in town. You forget how terrible it was just 4 months ago and then half way through your 2nd piece of pizza you remember.

Sometimes you may feel that you take 3 steps forward and then slide back a step or two. This is perfectly normal and no reason to condemn yourself. God is not condemning you. Remember that His goal is to rebuild the relationship with you that he had with Adam and Eve before the fall of man. He is patiently loving you and is able to carry you through the rough patches if you will allow him to do so.

Next you will need to write down how much time per week you would like to spend adding new experiences and learning who God wants to be in your life and who you are in Him. What classes or small groups can you join? What books would you like to read? Would you be willing to dedicate 30 minutes every day to reading something that will change your life? Write down your excuses for why your mind tells you that you can't do it. Fold up the piece of paper and burn it. Every time your mind gives you a reason why you can't do something and you believe the reason that it gave you, the lie will take hold and become truth in your mind. Your mind only knows what it has already experienced. Do not claim what your mind tells you as truth. Read, research, ask questions and ask God to lead you to find the real truth.

One other obstacle to remaining on the narrow path will be people who just don't understand what you are doing. There will be times when the narrow and wide paths cross and you will see your friends. You will see people from past and relationships that want to pull you back onto the wide path with them. As the old saying goes, misery definitely loves company.

The important part here is to make sure that you do not leave yourself a way to get off of the path. All bridges and boats that lead from one path to the other must be burned. When Cortez came to America and brought his forces on shore, they saw the jungles that they had to traverse and began to complain about how thick everything was and how difficult it was going to be to go forward. As they began to turn back they noticed that all of their ships were on fire. Cortez burned every ship as they watched and then reminded everyone that they only had one direction to go – Forward. What are your escape bridges and boats? Write them down and burn them. Do what needs to be done to make sure you can't go back to the people and places that keep you lost and searching for a way out.

As you embark on this journey to drink from the river peace and learning how to hear the voice of the Holy Spirit, the devil will be continually attacking you. He will remind you how inadequate you are, how you will never measure up, how stupid you are for doing this, and he will use other people to assist him in this cause. There is a fountain on this narrow path that you will be able to drink from that will be infinitely more satisfying than anything you can get to from your boat or bridge. When you believe that fountain is there and you desire to drink from it you will keep moving forward.

Once you let go of some unhealthy relationships and burn those bridges you are going to need some help. I love the story of the little girl who showed her parents a letter asking God to send her someone to be her friend. Her mom told her that God is your friend and he is with you always. The little girl replied "I know momma but I want someone with skin on them." This is a funny story but carries a lot of truth in the fact that we as humans are looking for other people to share our lives with. We feel connected when we feel that someone else is going through the same things that we are as we identify with their struggles and victories. So your homework assignment is to find someone else or a small group of people that are also on the narrow path. This is very important. Remember that most people are on the wide path and many of them will be used by the great deceiver to feed you lies and push you in the wrong direction.

National sales trainer Jim Rohn says that we are the average of the 5 people or sources with which we spend the most time. So if we spend our time with self-involved negative people what traits do you think we will exhibit? Internet, television programs, or people; it doesn't matter. In an effort to be accepted we emulate what we see and it becomes the norm. How do you think your life would change if your best friend was friendly, positive, genuine, loving and gave you affirmation and honesty? Sounds pretty nice, doesn't it? Ask God to bring that friend into your life and remove friends that are negative and bring you down. Maybe you can help that person in the future once you are in a better place but the goal for now is for you to learn how to walk in peace. Once you find peace you can assist others and be their guide as they learn to walk the narrow path.

Another mistake that is easy to make as you learn to let go is to attempt to maintain control of life by defining what we are willing to do or not do. We do this by making mental lists of things we want and things that we would like to happen. I call this forecasting and when we forecast our surrender we are still in control.

Here is a good example of how forecasting works. Let's say I am going out on a date with my spouse and I determine I would like that date to end in a romantic encounter. What I am going to experience on that date has now changed because I have predetermined what I would like the outcome to be. My attitude during the date will fluctuate based on her reaction to my advances.

The opposite would be for the date to progress organically

and spontaneously. We will both enjoy ourselves and be open to have fun no matter what because I do not have any expectations for what I have to do to make my will happen.

In the same way, we must step into our decision for wanting something different in our lives without deciding exactly what it is that we want. When I decide what I want to surrender, that is all I will see, and that is all I will be able to work on. Sort of like a murder investigation where the detectives only focus on one suspect so they miss out on the real killer who is right around the corner. They may even convict the wrong killer and not know for 20 years that they did the wrong thing because they chose who they were going to convict. Surrender does not involve me choosing what my surrender or new reality will look like. I only need to make the decision that I would like something different and lay myself at the feet of a living Christ.

The homework for this chapter will be to ask God to begin to reveal in you your new reality. For him to show you what it is that you've been holding on to and give you the strength to waive the white flag and let it go as He replaces it with your new reality. This reality does not need to be created. It already exists inside of you and is waiting to be awakened. Next, do not run from your brokenness! This is very important. Remember that peace is on the other side of our pain. If you run from the pain and seek to hide or dilute it then you will not find what you are looking for. Exist in your brokenness till God reveals in you your new identity.

The flesh still wants to be in control. Be aware of its attempts to come back in and take over.

Chapter 17
Redemption

And Then Life Kicked Him... Squarely in the Face

Brian!!! She shrieked at the top of her lungs. I was upstairs and she was down. The scream was terrifying as it ripped completely through my ears and into my heart. I bounded down the stairs 3 at a time with long strides from my now 6' 2" tall narrow frame. My hair was spiked higher than ever, probably more as an act of defiance to the church than to anyone else. It was Sunday morning and I had been upstairs getting ready to go to church when she screamed out for me. I tried really hard to want to go to church. Jennifer and I had gotten married and I had a family now so I tried my best to do what I had always been told were the right things to do.

The first thought to cross my mind was a nightmare. I had left Alissa sitting in the corner of the big chair downstairs. "There's no possible way she could have fallen out" I thought as I rounded the corner and headed through the kitchen for the next set of stairs. She was only 4 months old and not yet mobile enough or big enough to have moved that far and fallen off the chair.

Just two steps into my descent of large leaps down the stairs revealed the horrific and shocking nature of the situation. Jennifer was standing several feet away from the baby but looking backward into my eyes as I swooped down the stairs and across the den floor as if I were the hero coming to save the day. But no hero was to be helpful on this day. Events had been set into motion that were beyond human control. I was always in control. I always had the answers. I was always able to fix everything. And for the first time in my life I knew something was broken and I could not fix it.

Her eyes were pure panic and desperation as they called out to me for help and guidance. Both of her beautiful brown eyes were welled with tears of fear and panic. A single solitary tear had escaped her eye and was rolling down her soft ivory cheek. I saw the reason for her fear but didn't know how to respond. "Was it finally happening to me?" I wondered. "Was God finally paying his visit to pay me for all my crimes against humanity?" I felt the hotness on the back of my neck and the lump building in my throat. Punishment was finally here and it could be more than I wanted to pay.

My mind instantly flashed back to the events of last night. I had tried not to go but it seemed like so much fun. All my friends were going so it seemed ok. I could still smell the club on my skin and taste the sweetness of the tequila on the back of my tongue. I had told God I would be good. But I had failed. It was so much fun to be bad just one more time. Being good all the time is so hard to keep up. It was just one moment away. Why me God? Why come after me? I'm nobody. I'm insignificant. I thought I was off the grid – I should've never come back to church." My mind flew with question after question in rapid fire succession. Time stood completely still as my mind reeled back and forth trying to find some stable ground to land on.

My eyes were fixed squarely on Alissa as her body lurched violently out of control. I had seen someone have a seizure before and knew instantly what it was. Her tiny hands were balled up in little fists and raised above her head. Her eyes were rolled up into her head which arched backwards and shook violently. Her incredibly tiny and fragile body coursed out of control in a scene of pure disbelief. I knelt down and gently put my arms around her as if to somehow stabilize the miniaturized version of myself. I held her there for what seemed like an eternity. Jennifer's cries could be heard in the background and added to the hopelessness of the situation. "What do we do?" She petitioned tearfully. "How do we make her stop?" I started to remember the last time I felt this helpless on the roof of my house at 10 years old but the memory escaped quickly. Instead the only emotions that came to visit me were my oldest and dearest friends – indifference and rage. Those memories had been deemed not safe and had to be locked away deep inside the impenetrable fortress never to be accessed again. The best way to live normally was to forget. A great chasm existed between me and my memories of childhood. At times I could see the memories off in the distance. They seemed to dance and play in far off fields of sunshine and flowers only to fall off a sheer jagged cliff that fell into a gnarled patch of briars. My memories lay entangled in the thorns and could only escape to come visit in my dreams. At night they were released to wreak havoc on my subconscious.

"She will stop soon" I assured her as if I knew for sure and an old familiar mantra from long ago crept slowly back into my mind. "I'm sorry I was bad. I won't do it again. I'll be a good boy." Make her stop shaking and I'll be a good boy. I promise."

After what seemed like an eternity of chaotic bedlam, the shaking subsided and the tiny child lay completely still as she slumped into a quiet, unresponsive sleep. Her chest moving softly in and out was the only remaining indicator of life. I gently handed her to Jennifer and quickly reached for the phone to call for help. I quickly called the man I idolized most. I called my father.

I called my father often, mostly in continuance of my lifelong attempts at being accepted by him. I always worked longer and harder than everyone else – always trying to prove to dad that I was a truly a man's man. The memories of childhood had faded and now only existed in my mind as the process of how a real man is made. The man making process was beginning again with my own son who was now just approaching two and a half years old. Nathan was a kind and affectionate boy who had been, in my opinion, a little to coddled by his mother and grandmother. He was fair haired and gentle minded with a great need for some toughening up. And lucky enough -or not- for him I had been trained in the art of making a tough man.

All memories of anything dad had done in the past were covered by layers of fog produced mostly in an effort to cope with the hazard that was my life. The memories often attempted to peer through the haze and contact the outer world but never seemed to be able to break completely through. Bits and pieces of images could be seen but were immediately pulled back into the deep dark depths of my mind. And so my mind created a new reality within itself with dad as the hero – the greatest man who ever lived and the creator of a man's man. But once the lie was started it grew and took root in the subconscious, until the lie became easier to believe than the truth and the truth became lost in a torrent of unseen wind and waves.

As Jennifer bundled up our tiny child, I was on the phone frantically yelling instructions to dad's secretary. "Alissa has had a seizure and we are going to the Hospital. Tell dad to meet us there." My mind raced with doom and gloom scenarios. "She is so tiny, what if she dies. Is she going to be ok?" But scenarios quickly turned to blame and the tormentor in my mind was there to take over. The tormentor visited often. He was wicked and cruel and seemed to have only one job – to remind me of who I was and what I had done.

"You know it's your fault Brian."

"That's not true. It was just a couple of drinks with friends." I didn't kill anybody."

"All sins are the same Brian so you might as well have killed someone. It's all the same to God. You got drunk and this is your punishment."

"Don't take it out on her. Please, I'll do anything if you'll make her be ok. She's so little, she didn't do anything wrong, I did."

"You've been doing wrong your whole life and now it's time to pay for it."

"I was just having some fun. I just wanted to be accepted by someone just one time in this God forsaken world. Tequila accepts me for who I am and never, ever rejects me."

"Tequila is evil and so are you. Nothing you can do will ever change that."

"I can be better. I can do more. I promise I will. Make her better and I will do more. I will do better."

"It's too late Brian. Your punishment has begun and she has to suffer because of you."

But this was not a fight that could be won. I wondered if I was alone in my fight or if others experienced this same type of internal quarreling. Tequila helped to quite the voice of the tormentor with its soft smooth and sultry demeanor. Her voice was that of goddess and siren rolled into one. She alone could quiet the voice and bring sleep to my mind.

The lines on the road sped past at great speed as we headed for the hospital. Alissa was still asleep in her post seizure comatose state. "Would God really punish my helpless infant for my sins?" I wondered almost aloud. The stories of God's punishment from church rang over and over in my mind.

"God must be an angry and vengeful God to come after such a little girl."

"He is angry. You have been rebellious your whole life and now it's time to pay the piper."

The doctors went to work quickly on Alissa who now being

wide awake screamed at the top of her lungs with every poke and prod. I sat outside on a small bench and stared at the sky. With each second that passed everything was changing. As a child I remembered how vivid and bright the world looked. How colors seemed so tasty you could almost eat them. The world used to be chocolaty and fruity and minty as each color combined to somehow form themselves into a savory delicacy that rolled off the back of the tongue. The colors which as a child seemed so vivid and bright had steadily faded year by year and now threatened to disappear forever. The blue sky slowly turned to pale gray and a shadow began to form in my heart and soul. The shadow cast its darkness in every direction until flowers no longer looked pretty. Everything was slowly turning the perceived color of my heart – a pale muted tone of black mixed with several boring tones of solid gray.

Your homework for this chapter is to identify the soundtrack that plays in your mind. The condemning voice knows your past and thus knows exactly where to go to turn your heart and mind away from God. The deceiver used my religious experience to make me believe that God was punishing me and doing this to my daughter. This caused me to hate God and Christians for many years. Spend some time thinking about your inner soundtrack and write down the condemning thoughts that play in your mind. Once you are aware of what they are you can see where they originated and then you can deal with how to reject the lies and keep them from defining who you are and who you will become.

Chapter 18
Revelation
Step 4 - But I Thought I Knew Who I Was

Why don't we do a quick recap of the steps we've covered already? Step 1 – Pain or discomfort in remaining the same. We have to dislike where we are in life enough to want to change it. Step 2 – Brokenness – It hurts and I can't fix it. I have to know that my life cannot be repaired in my power. Step 3 – Decide that you would like something different. I make the decision that I would like something different with my life and this desire will kindle a fire in my heart and mind to head down a different path. And that leads us to step 4 – Reboot my hard drive. No I haven't lost my mind just yet. In this step, understanding how our brain can work like a computer will help us to set the stage for true change and not just a change in our behavior. As we discussed previously, many times we focus on removing or refining our bad habits which will work for a time but cannot be maintained indefinitely.

Our ultimate goal in this step is to remove all preconceived ideas, beliefs and ways of thinking from my past. To accomplish this it will be beneficial to think about our brain as a computer. As we go through life the brain is constantly gathering and storing information just like the hard drive on a computer. It is the job of our mind to then take the information that the brain gathers and to figure out what it all means and draw conclusions.

Events that happen in our lives are meaningless until the mind gets involved and tells us what to believe about the event. Let me explain. Let's say that your best friend doesn't show up for your birthday party. The fact that they didn't show up is just a fact with no meaning at all. Your mind gives that event meaning by telling you that she must not care about you at all. If she didn't come to my party then she isn't really my best friend. The mind can also take it a step further to define what that event says about you. I must not be very important to her. Maybe I'm not important to anyone. This concept is laid out in detail by James B. Richards in his book How to Stop the Pain.

Once the mind has helped you draw several different possible conclusions it will begin to draw up the framework for how you should respond to this situation and similar situations in the future. The new framework for this situation would most likely be that she is not my friend anymore and for the foreseeable future, I will refuse to talk to her. The course of the future has now been changed because of the assessment and decisions my mind made from this single event.

The body will now act on what the mind has decided. The mind decided that she doesn't care about me so we aren't going to talk to her anymore and so the body carries out the minds wishes. The next time I see her I am giving her the cold shoulder and she better not dare try to call me because I'm not answering. This whole process is now our new identity. We are not friends anymore. Something fundamental has changed inside of me.

So that leads us to a new understanding of what identity is. Our identity is who we believe we are based on the framework created by the mind because of experiences from the past. Let me say that again because this is a very important truth to let sink in. Our identity is who we believe we are based on the framework created by the mind because of experiences from the past. If we can realize that this process is happening over and over and day after day, we will then have the ability to stop the process mid flow.

Let's dig a little deeper because this is a real life changing, or should I say, mind changing concept to adopt. The most important part to realize is that it is who we believe we are and not necessarily who we actually are. As we talked about in an earlier chapter, when we are adamant about what we believe, we don't leave room for the possibility that we may not have all of the information necessary to make the right call. In the previous analogy I may not know that my friend was having an emergency meeting with her lawyer for her bankruptcy that she has been too embarrassed to tell me about.

But the true root of the problem isn't actually that my friend missed my party at all. To recognize the root we need to look at why we got upset that they missed the party in the first place. We generally get upset because something happened that we didn't approve of. The world has really worked a number on our minds in the process of really making us believe that everything is about us and everything is supposed to happen a certain way. And so we end up taking offense to everything that everyone does that doesn't happen the way that we think it is supposed to happen.

Let me tell you a story about a group of teens that I once worked with on a project and two of the girls who were best friends weren't talking to each other. Throughout the day I noticed them giving each other really nasty looks. I pulled one of them to the side and asked her what was wrong. She said that her former best friend was now going out with her ex-boyfriend. She admitted that they had been broken up for several months now so I asked her why she was upset. She said this is something that you just don't do. From that moment on it didn't matter what I asked her about the situation. She was holding to the belief that this wasn't right and she was not going to talk to either of them ever again. She lost a best friend because of this belief that was planted by the high school girl rulebook. As we look at this we may chuckle a little bit as we remember things like this from high school, but how many people do you know that are still mentally stuck in a high school type of mentality? Have you looked at yourself to see how many beliefs and reactions exist in your life that have you perpetually stuck in high school? I think I feel a homework assignment coming on.

So how do we begin the process of rebooting the hard drive in our minds to remove the absolutes that exist? How do we remove absolutes that we really don't even know are in our minds? The process begins by changing all of our absolute opinions to flexible opinions. In the story from above, had the young girl believed that it was ok for her best friend and her ex-boyfriend to be happy together than she would not have reacted the way she did. Conflict would have been removed and she would have kept a few good friends. This means that peace could have existed if she could have changed what she believed. The best part is that she never once would have had to work on her behavior because a change in belief leads to a change in behavior.

The key to changing these beliefs is going to be awareness. Every time we see or feel ourselves reacting to anything, we can stop and see if the belief that is driving the reaction is based on truth, or on the non-existent high school playbook. Some of our beliefs may even be going back to the middle school playbook so make sure you dig deep. Also, watch for statements of opinion that you make on a routine basis. Statements that begin with "I always" and "I never" will keep us stuck in those old playbooks for many years.

In my life I have adopted a policy to help make sure that I allow for the chance that I may not be right when I am speaking my opinion. I do not use the words always and never and when speaking my opinion, I do not produce it as fact. I will add the phrase "in my opinion" to any infinite statement to remove any adamancy and allow for the chance that new information may arise that may cause me to change my opinion. This also accomplishes the task of making sure that I maintain a flexible identity. What I know in life can change at any moment in time based on a new event and/or new information.

The formula that controls this way of thinking is Experiences → Belief → How We Act. When I have an experience my mind will determine what it wants to believe and it will tell my body how to act. This is why our homework from a few chapters ago was so important. We listed events from our past and present in which we have experienced brokenness. Each one of these events was an experience that led to a belief and ultimately shaped how we act.

Our next step then becomes to ask the Holy Spirit to reveal in us a new reality and to help us let go of the false identities that have been created in our lives. If we do not remove the old identity, then this causes one identity to be written directly over another. This is why we see people who are in churches doing good work but still making a mess by casting judgment and offending others, all the while believing they are in the right. They have an identity crisis. Let me show you what it looks like when you write one identity over another.

Looks like a big mess doesn't it? This can actually be a really good self-checkpoint for us. If I see myself acting out in any area I can look to see what event took place and ask "Because of that event, what am I believing about myself?" Once I find the belief that emanated from the event I can choose not to believe what my mind is trying to tell me. This may sound complex and difficult at first but I promise you that once you start doing it you will see a definite difference and with practice and repetition it becomes easier and easier.

As new events happen in my life I need to be aware that each event has the capacity to either create a brand new belief or simply re-affirm a belief from the past. If someone else sets an appointment with me and then blows me off, my mind may try again to tell me that I must not be important. It is my choice to believe and act out of that belief, or reject it and choose to believe that I am valuable regardless of whether someone came to my party or not.

Let's do a quick recap to make sure that we have this important concept committed to memory so that we can catch this process as it happens in real time in our lives.

1. The brain gathers and stores information
2. The mind draws conclusions from that information
3. The mind decides what to believe
4. The body acts out of what the mind believes
5. We must question every belief and look for the truth

I remember walking into a church during my agnostic years and hearing the speaker reading out of an NIV Bible. I turned to my wife and told her that we had to leave because they were reading out of the wrong Bible. I heard a voice in my head ask me a question. You don't even believe in me and yet you are going to tell others which version of my book to read. Amazing isn't it. A lie was planted in my core so deep that I didn't believe in God but I was ready to walk out of a church over them doing something that I was taught was wrong back in elementary school.

Question everything! The truth exists but cannot be written on top of something else. The hard drive must be rebooted and all preconceived ideas, beliefs and absolute ways of thinking removed. Once it has been removed God can reveal in us our true identity. It is a beautiful thing to start to discover who you truly are as God reveals it to you one little piece at a time. Be prepared for it to trickle in one or two pieces at a time and do not get in a hurry. This type of work can be so emotional that if He did it all at once I think we would explode! Let it happen as it happens.

Your homework for this week will be to ask God to open your mind to see absolute ideas that exist in your mind. Be looking for absolute beliefs about yourself, about the way life works, and about God. Look for ideas that keep you from learning or seeing the truth because your belief is so set and engrained in your mind. As they are revealed to you, write them in your journal and ask God to help you remove the lie and replace it with His truth on the matter.

The two most important preconceptions to consider will be who you think you are – your identity, and who you think God is – concept of God. These two are very closely connected. Who you think God is will determine who you are. Until you are open to allow Him to reveal who He is in your life you will not be able to see who you are. In order to be open to allow Him to have that freedom to work in your life you will have to start to see the truth about who He says He is and not who you grew up believing He was. Trust in Him says that I believe You have my best interest at heart and I am willing to let go of who I think I am so that You can have free reign to reveal in me who You are and who You created me to be. Be honest with yourself and honest with God on this step. Lay it all out there or you will only scratch the surface of the places God wants to go in your heart. Remember, if an absolute exists, the area of my life that it occupies cannot be changed.

Chapter 19
Redemption

9-11-2001 – Need I say more...

Most of us remember vividly that dark infamous day when The Twin Towers of The World Trade Center fell. Most could tell you exactly where they were and what they stopped doing to sit and watch, horrified at the events unfolding. A very surreal moment for every one of us sitting on the edge of our seats wondering what was going to happen next. Watching the carnage unfold right before our eyes and wondering how many people were trapped inside the towers and how many were already dead. I sat there and watched both towers fall. I sat there and let my heart fill with anger towards anyone who could perpetrate such an evil attack against defenseless people. And then just like every other day... I went to work.

Deep inside I was bothered by what happened but I didn't really know how to process what I was feeling. I was so detached from feeling that most anyone I knew could die right in front of me and I would have expected it to happen so I wouldn't be sad. I always seemed to be ready for God to come along and take away anything I loved so I never let myself love anything. The only thing I truly loved was Jennifer but I was so messed up that I didn't know how to show her real love. I was totally prepared at any moment of any day for God to strike anyone I knew dead, just for being close to me. So I couldn't let anyone too close. Everyone I knew assumed I was happy because I knew how to put a smile on my face. I knew how to laugh and was really good at being the life of the party when I wanted to. But no one really knew the darkness that lay deep inside my soul except for Jennifer.

So I just focused on my work. Of course, I had to prove to dad that I was a man and so that's what I did. I owned my first company at 16 years old building swimming pools across the southeast as a subcontractor with my 2 brothers. We would show up to build a pool and people would ask, "How old are y'all?" "Old enough to know how to build a pool but we may have to stop and change our youngest brother's diaper," I would say with a big grin on my face.

When I got married I was working over 100 hours a week and I cut back to 90 as a wedding present. "You have to make hay while the sun shines" I would always say. At 23 I started selling real estate and pushed my way up to the multi-million dollar club within 2 years. Because I had been working since I was 8 years old, that really was all I knew how to do. I worked to give my life meaning and purpose and most of the time would work a 7 day work week. I drew my self-worth from being the best at what I did and became so focused on being the best that I often lost track of time. I would forget what time it was and fail to go home or even call to say I was late. I was in a word – emotionless. The only true emotion that I carried was buried deep within and threatened at times to pour out on anyone who dared to press my buttons. Rage – I held within my soul a silent rage at all the forces of heaven or hell that were at work on this out of control chaotic planet.

And buttons – let's not even get started on my buttons. Let's just call them issues or maybe little idiosyncrasies. Those are the nice terms. I was an all in all sure enough freak. If there was a label you could pin it on me – OCD, ADD, Hyper-focus Disorder, Germophobia – just to name the big ones. At this point I had gone almost a few years without stepping on any sidewalk cracks or touching anyone other than my immediate family. Not to mention that I couldn't touch any items in public. I was terrified of getting sick and tried to control everything. I had taken the chaos I had grown up with and tried to turn it into order. Anything that could be controlled, I would control it to the nth degree. I could control what I touched and how everything on my desk was at 45 or 90 degree angles.

So when an event like 9-11 comes along it shakes the very fabric of control. It is a stark reminder that there are things that are beyond our control. This type of reminder is cruel and unnerving in a world in which I am god, king, judge and jury.

When I got to work that day the water cooler talk was at full speed. Did you see the towers fall? We need to attack whoever did this? How many people do you think were inside?

Next I had to listen to the Christians in all their piety tell all of us lesser people why this evil had befallen us. But as it turns out, they were torn as to who should be to blame. Half of the people said that this was definitely the work of the devil and the other half said that it was the punishment from an Almighty God for the country that had turned its back on Him. I instantly pounced on the opportunity for mockery. So let me get this straight. Half of you say the devil did it, and half of you say that God did it. Maybe y'all should get together in a committee and see if you can decide whose fault it is. When you come up with who is to blame let me know so I can give him a piece of my mind. I laughed till I cried as they all tried to explain their points of view, each one not realizing that their points are biased by whatever their parents or preacher taught them. Each one thinking they are so right and everyone else is so wrong. The piety, the hypocrisy, the self-righteousness – it all really got to me. It took me right back to 6 years old and the old deacons smacking me on the back of the head for anything that wasn't good enough or didn't meet their standards. "Stop running in church boy this is the house of God." I still have flashbacks when I see anyone in a suit on a Sunday.

That night I went to bed clearly confused about the events of the day. Jennifer and I laid awake discussing everything we had taken in over the course of the last 12 hours - the collapse of the buildings and several thousand dead including the rescuers who were crushed by the falling towers; the talk of God and punishment weaved together with the devil and his dominion over the earth. It seemed so overwhelming. How do you make sense of a God that would pull out his giant hammer and smash anything he doesn't like? How do you make sense of a little girl who is having hundreds of seizures per day and a family that lives half of their life in the hospital?

This is usually the point in my mind when the glaze comes in to wipe all thoughts away into nothingness. A few shots of tequila and it all goes away. No feelings, no remorse, no thinking. We are all just floating around on a breeze and we are left here to fend for ourselves. If there is a God who created us He surely doesn't care about us and can't change anything because the devil must surely be in control. My current view is very agnostic in nature and is getting very close to atheism.

But for some reason this night was different. I was tired of not knowing what to believe. I was tired of not knowing what was out there. If there was something to believe in I wanted to believe in it. So I did what I usually do, I hung it all out there and went for the fences. I gave God an ultimatum. As I stared at the ceiling for what seemed like hours I finally said "God, If your there, if you do exist, then you have one week to show me that you are there. At the end of one week, if you don't show me that you exist, I will never speak your name again. I will be an atheist!"

Now I've heard many people say that you should never give God an ultimatum, but I believe what I did was activate

God's promise of, "Ask and you will receive, seek and you will find, knock and the door will be opened." I directly asked God for information about him and in doing so knocked on a door that would change the course of my entire life.

Your homework for this chapter is to activate your promise from God. Spend some time in quiet and take a knock on His door.

Chapter 20
Revelation

False Beliefs

As we discussed earlier, our beliefs will control how we act. So what are some examples of false beliefs that may be at work in our lives and how do we find the truth to remove those beliefs? In Anne Trippe's book called Marriage, The Journey she reviews several different lies that exist in relationships and looks to scripture for the truth to change the belief and ultimately how we will act. I would also like for you to notice that when a false belief is active in your life how it controls what you will do and what you cannot do.

Let's look at an example. Belief – I must control everything to make sure that I am safe. If this is my belief than everything I do will be towards that end and I will be completely justified with anything that I do to meet that end, no matter who gets hurt in the process or how it gets done. What is the truth though? Once we begin to trust that God has our best interest at heart again we will be able to find truth in the words that He left for us.

He tells us in his Word, "*I am secure because I am hidden with Christ in God*." When I believe the truth that God has given me in His word, I am able to let go of the control that I exhibit in different areas of my life that I was previously unable to release. What we believe controls what we will do. If I believe God and trust that everything that He does in my life is for my best interest no matter what and that He has a plan for exactly what He wants to happen, whether good or bad, then and only then can I release control and be at peace.

Here is another good one. Belief – I must perform perfectly and avoid mistakes in order to be acceptable. How many of us had a parent that drove this one home for us on a daily basis. How many of us are now a parent that is passing this belief on to our children? So what does God say is the truth? *"I am perfect in Christ; one spirit with Him. I have been made accepted by Him."* The truth is that if I believe that there is nothing I can do to make God love me more or less, than I no longer have to perform for anyone's acceptance. So many people are trapped in what I like to call vending machine Christianity. If I want something from God I have to put some money or service into the machine to get what I want out of it. My belief that I am perfect and I am accepted by Him releases me from that bondage to servitude and I can now serve because it is in my heart to do so. Now anything that I choose to do to serve Him or anyone else can be done knowing that there is no expectation or pressure for me to perform. When I know that I am loved by Him I no longer have to perform for that love and acceptance.

How about this one? Belief – I cannot have peace or contentment if my loved one doesn't change. This one is very heavy. Many times we will attempt to draw life from someone who we are very close with but they just don't ever seem to measure up. We look at them and say "I hurt" and we expect them to fix it for us. Maybe they keep messing up and letting us down and we keep looking to them to make everything ok in our lives. For many years I had this expectation on my wife. The weight of this expectation wore heavy upon her until she could not bear it any more. Who are you looking to? Who has to change for you to be ok and what is the truth from God? *"Christ is my peace. He alone gives me peace. When I cease from my own way, I have rest. When I humble myself I will delight in an abundance of peace."*

The entire list of false beliefs and the truth used to counter each one is listed below. When I first read this list I reviewed each one of these common false beliefs and circled over 20 that were active in my life. I then carried the list with me to make sure that every time I realized that I might be acting out of one of them I could read the truth and quickly counteract the effects of believing the lie. Review the following list of beliefs below and circle which ones are active in your life. And then keep the list close be able to access the truth when you need it.

If you are not yet to the point where you can trust these words from God as the truth, that is ok. This is an exercise that we can come back to at a later time once we have had the opportunity to better address our mistrust or anger with God. If you are somewhat on the fence, then what have you got to lose by introducing a new way of thinking? Give it a try and see how it feels to think thoughts based on something new.

False Belief	**Truth**
1. I must control circumstances for me (and my family) to be secure.	I am secure because I am hidden with Christ in God. *Col. 3:3 - All my needs are supplied in Christ. Phil. 4:19 - It is not by my power nor strength, but by His Spirit. Zech. 4:6 - He is a shield to those who walk uprightly.*
2. I must perform perfectly and avoid mistakes to be acceptable.	I am perfect in Christ; one spirit with Him. *Heb.10:14; I Cor. 6:17 - I have been made accepted by Him. Eph 1:6 - Christ died that I would be the righteousness of God in Him.*

False Belief	Truth
3. I am responsible for my spouse's or another's emotional well-being. I must apologize if he or she isn't ok or if they do something wrong. I am accountable to God for my spouse.	Each one shall give account of himself to God. *Rom. 14:12 - I cannot rescue my brother by any means. Ps. 49:7 - Each person eats the fruit of his own way. Pr. 1:31*
4. I must stay emotionally guarded to be safe and secure.	The Lord is my safety. *Ps. 4:8; 27: 1-6; 32:7-11 - Safety is only of the Lord. Pr. 1:33; 3:23; 21:31 - As I trust Christ. His peace will guard my heart and mind. Phil. 4:7 - He is my shield and fortress. Ps. 18:1-3*
5. I must be strong and independent to survive.	Christ's strength is perfect in my weakness. *II Cor. 12:9 - My life is to be dependent on Christ, since He is the Vine and I am a branch in Him. Without Him I can do nothing. John 15:5; II Cor. 12:10*
6. I do not measure up. I am not worthy of love and I may deserve to be punished.	Christ has made me accepted in Him. *Eph. 1 6; Ps. 139:13-18 - I am chosen, righteous, holy, a saint: A new creation. II Cor. 5:17; I Peter 2:9; I Cor. 1:2*

False Belief	Truth
7. Real men do not show they need help.	When I humble myself before God, in due time He exalts me. *I Peter 5:6 - Pride comes before a fall. Pr. 16:18*
8. I must achieve to gain significance and confidence.	My confidence is to be in the Lord. Not in myself. *Pro. 3:26: 14:26 - I am to put no confidence in my flesh. Phil. 3:3 - I am to humble myself and become of no reputation. Phil. 2:5-8.*
9. I must get respect from my mate and others to know I am of worth.	I am called to love and to serve others and consider them better than myself. *Phil. 2:3 – Pride comes before destruction and shame. Pr. 16:18; 11:21 – I am to become of no reputation and be a servant. Phil. 2:5-8 – He has made me accepted and perfect.*
10. I must be heard and/ or right to know I am of value to my loved one or others	I am not to be wise in my own eyes. *Pr. 3:7 - I am to find my value in Christ. Eph. 1:6 - See #9*

False Belief	Truth
11. I must "fix and direct" if things are to go right for me and if I am going to be ok. I must control interactions and circumstances.	God will work all things together for good for me if I love Him and am called according to His purpose. *Rom. 8:28 - He is faithful and will cause it to happen. I Thess. 5:24 - God works His will in the army of heaven and among the inhabitants of the earth. Dan. 4:35 - God will accomplish that which concerns me. Ps. 138:8*
12. I must be the best to find worth and security.	The least shall be the greatest. *Luke 9:48 - God is my worth, security, my shield and fortress. See # 17. Pr: 2:7b - Safety is of the Lord. Pr. 21:31; Jer. 16:19*
13. Emotions represent truth.	Jesus Christ said He is the Truth. Emotions do not represent truth and are not to be trusted. *John 14:6*
14. My peace is tied to my spouse's and/or others' opinions and to my being treated fairly. I am entitled to my spouse treating me the way the Lord commands him/her to, so I will be fulfilled.	Jesus Christ is my peace and gives me peace. *John 14:2 - I am in perfect peace as my mind is fixed on Him. As I humble myself, I will enjoy peace. Ps. 37:11; Is. 26:3 See # 32, 37*

False Belief	Truth
15. Husbands & wives should complete each other.	Each has been made complete in Christ. *Col. 2:10*
16. Others and losses are responsible for my pain. My emotional well-being or lack of it is somebody else's fault or responsibility.	I am responsible to receive and walk in the healing, recovery, comfort, peace and restoration from Christ. *Is. 61:la-3; 58:8a; 54:1-14; Ps. 23:3*
17. I must prove I am right to know I am of worth.	Christ has made me accepted in Him. *Eph. 1:6; #9, #10 Ps. 139:13-18 - I am chosen, righteous, holy, a saint: A new creation. II Cor. 5:17; I Peter 2:9; I Cor. 1:2*
18. I can't help being depressed and without hope if my circumstances don't change.	Christ is my defender and my justifier. *Rom. 5:1; Col. 3:3; Isa. 54:17; Ps. 91:11; Acts 13:39 -God will make my enemies to be at peace with me when my way pleases Him. Pr. 16:7*
19. I must explain, justify and defend myself. I must please my spouse and /or others to avoid rejection and find acceptance.	There is no condemnation to me as I walk after the Spirit. Christ came to make me perfect in my conscience. *Jn. 3:18; Rom. 8:1; Heb. 9:9,14 - I am forgiven of all my sins. Col. 2:13*

False Belief	Truth
20. I must live under the burden of guilt if another isn't ok or if I have failed or sinned.	I must put no confidence in human flesh. *Phil. 3: 3*
21. I can't be O.K. unless I can trust my loved one.	Birth determines my identity. I have been made a new creation by my new birth. The old me died with Christ. *Gal. 2:20; II Cor. 5:17*
22. What I do makes me who I am.	Birth determines my identity. I have been made a new creation by my new birth. The old me died with Christ. *Gal. 2:20; II Cor. 5:17*
23. I must live in shame from abuse in my early years. It affects my life and I can't get over it.	As I trust Christ, I will forget the shame of my youth. Instead of shame, He will give me double honor. He came to heal my broken heart and give beauty for ashes. He will restore the years the locusts have eaten. My recovery will spring forth quickly. *Is.58:8a; Is.61:1a,3,7; 54:4-8*
24. I am inadequate.	I have been made adequate. *II Cor. 3:5-6 - I can do all things through Christ. I am complete in Him. Col. 2:10. Phil. 4:13 - He makes me adequate. Heb.13:21 See #34.*

False Belief	Truth
25. I can't have any peace or contentment if my loved one doesn't change.	Christ is my peace. He gives me peace. *John 14:27 - When I cease from my own way, I have rest. Heb. 4:10 - Peace is mine through Christ. John 14:27 - When I humble myself, I will delight in an abundance of peace. Ps. 37:1*
26. I can't help being anxious when the future is uncertain.	As I humble myself and cast my fears on God, He will exalt me in due time. *I Peter 5:6-7 - I am to be anxious for nothing. Phil. 4:6 – God will preserve and sustain me as I trust Him. Ps. 16:8-9 Ps. 23:4 - The Lord preserves those who love Him. Ps. 3:23; 145:2; Prov. 2:8 - I am not to be afraid, for I dwell in the shelter of the Most High God. Ps. 91:5-6,10; Ps. 18:1-3 - So I am not to be troubled nor fearful. John 14:27*
27. I cannot be happy if I do not get my needs of worth and security met by my spouse or another.	He shall supply ALL my needs according to His riches in glory by Christ Jesus. *Phil. 4:19 (See all of the above.)*

False Belief	Truth
28. The Lord has never cared enough about me to answer my prayers.	If I abide in Him. I can ask and it will be given. *Jo. 15:7 - If I ask and don't receive in God's timing, I have asked out of the wrong motive. James 4:2-3; I Jn. 3:22; 5:14*
29. If the Lord wanted good things for me, He wouldn't have allowed so much loss and pain.	Tribulation and trials will come to all, beginning with God's people. But Christ has overcome these things on my behalf. *I Peter 1:6: 4:12; Jn 16:33 - He has plans for my good, and desires to satisfy me with good things. Jer. 29:11; Ps. 103:5a - After I have experienced a trial, trusting Him, He will establish, strengthen and perfect me. I Peter 5:10*
30. If the Lord cared about me, He would give me a person to fill my loneliness or make me complete and fulfilled. I need a person to complete me.	I will remain lonely unless I die to my own way of trying to make things work for me. *Jn. 12:24 - He wants to fill me and my loneliness with Himself. I am to find my completeness in Christ. Col. 3:3; Eph. 5:17,18*

False Belief	Truth
31. I must punish those who have done me wrong. Sometimes punishing my spouse or others will make them give me what I need.	God will avenge, vindicate me. I must release others from what they owe so that I won't suffer tormenting emotions. *Rom. 12:19: Heb. 10:30-31; Matt. 18:23-35*
32. My worth and value should come from hard work and responsibility.	My value and worth are only found in who Christ has made me – not in my performance. Christ has made me accepted in Him. *Eph. 1:6; Ps. 139:13-18 - My confidence is to be in the Lord, not myself. Pro. 3:26; 14:26; I am to put no confidence in my flesh. Phil. 3:3*
33. My security and value should come from my loved one protecting and providing for me or doing certain things for me.	The Lord in me is my provider, my security, my worth. He preserves me as I walk in faith. *Ps. 31:23; 145:20; 97:10; Pr. 2:8; Also see #17, #4*
34. I should find significance from another's love, appreciation, and acceptance. I must have everyone's love and approval to feel good about myself and be emotionally ok.	See #35. I am not entitled to others meeting my needs. My needs are to be met in Christ. I am complete in Him. He will fill me. *Phil. 4:19: Col. 2:10: Eph. 5:17-18*

False Belief	Truth
35. Satisfaction and fulfillment should come from my marital partner.	The Lord will satisfy my hungry soul as I walk in Him. *Is. 58:10 - He will fill me with His Spirit. Eph.5: 17-18*
36. I am not blessed if God doesn't give me the things I want, according to my reason and timing. Things must go my way for me to be happy and satisfied.	God's ways are higher than my ways. He is in control, and works all things together for my good if I love Him and am called according to His purpose. As I trust God and do not lean on my own understanding, He will direct my paths. *Pr. 3:5; Rom. 8:28 - He has plans for my good. to give me hope and a future. Jer. 29:11 - Only He knows the times and seasons under His authority.*
37. I must earn any good thing to enjoy from God.	He has freely given me all things to enjoy. I am justified freely by His grace. *Rom. 3:24; I Cor. 2:12; I Tim. 6:17; Matt. 10:8*
38. I must have everyone's love and approval to feel good about myself and be ok emotionally.	See # 35, #37, #38. I can't count on others approval for meeting my needs of worth, validation and significance. These needs are met in Christ.

False Belief	Truth
39. I must struggle to surrender or put away the flesh (my old "survival strategies").	I must not try to put them away. If my mind is set on the Spirit. I will enjoy life and peace. When I just cease from my own works, then I will have rest and peace. When I abide in Christ, I have joy *Jn.15:11; Heb. 4:10 - As I walk after the Spirit, abiding and focusing on the Spirit, I won't fulfill the desires of the flesh. Gal. 5:16*
40. Life must be fair for me to be calm. I am a victim and cannot be ok until I am no longer victimized.	Life is not fair. Trials and injustices will come to all. I enter into Christ's victory as I take up the trial (cross) daily and deny myself. I cannot follow Christ unless I do this. Calmness and peace are found only in Christ. *See #31, #14, Matt. 16:24,14:33*
41. My childhood issues must be dealt with before I can be ok.	My issues *have* been dealt with because I have died with Christ and am a new creation. I am ok when I recognize that He has given me the victory & cease from my struggling. *See #34, #22. Heb. 4:10*

False Belief	Truth
42. If I punish my spouse or others, then they will love me and give me what I need.	I will eat the fruit of my own way. I will reap what I sow. If I sow to the flesh, I will reap corruption. As I am unselfish and love my spouse and others (sow to the spirit), I will reap that eternal life of Christ's sufficiency for me. *Matt. 5:46: Gal. 6:7,8: Prov. 1:31*
43. Love must be earned. I must perform to certain standards for God to accept me and to be loved and accepted by others. I must know I am loved by, and important to another to be ok.	God loved me, chose me and accepted me by His grace while I was a sinner. He freely gives me all things to enjoy. He has made me accepted in Him. I do not have to have acceptance from a person for my needs to be met. All my needs are met in Christ. *See #40, #2. In 15:13; Phil.4:19*
44. I should not have adversity or opposition in life, relationships or marriage.	I know that trials come to all and I should not be surprised when they come. God allows them to happen so that I won't depend on myself but on God. *II Cor. 1:9; See #29, #31*

False Belief	Truth
45. Others are to blame and are responsible for how I feel. It is someone's fault. I am a victim.	I am responsible for me. See #3 **He** came to restore and heal my broken soul. *Luke 4:18. See #16, #18, #26, #45.*

Hopefully now you have at least identified the major false beliefs that exist in your life. The next list we want to look at is a list of false beliefs toward God. There are so many things that can cloud how we see God. Many times we will see God through the lens that we see our father or predominant parent. As you can imagine I initially believed that God was a controlling egomaniac waiting for me to mess up so he could smash me underneath his giant hammer. Complete the worksheet below to take a look at how you really see God. Be completely honest. God can handle it. He already knows your answers anyway. He just wants you to know them so that the two of you can get it all out on the table and He can reveal the truth about Himself to you.

1. When I think about being with God, I feel...?

2. When I have to trust God, I feel...?

3. When I think about God, I wish...?

4. Sometimes I get angry with God when...?

5. I really enjoy God when...?

6. The one thing I would change about myself to please God is...?

7. When I think about God's commands I feel...?

8. I feel angry toward God when...?

9. Sometimes I wish God would...?

10. I can really depend on God when...?

11. The one thing that frustrates me most about God is...?

12. The one thing that frightens me about God is...?

13. The one thing that bothers me most about God is...?

14. The one thing I am afraid God will do is...?

The above questions are printed by permission from Grace Fellowship International ©1987.

Now that you have aired things out with God let's take a look at what He says is the truth about himself as we contrast it with false beliefs about Him. Circle the ones that you believe are active in your life.

False Belief About God	Truth
God is distant and disinterested in me.	God is intimate and involved in my life – Ps. 139:1-18 He indwells me. I Cor. 3:16; Rom. 8:11 - By His mercy and grace, and because it pleased Him to do so. God chose me to be His child while I was a sinner, and unrighteous. This is an unconditional gift. Eph.1:4, 2:5;Rom. 3:24: II Thess. 2:13:
God is insensitive and uncaring.	God is kind and compassionate – Ps. 103:8-14 He has forgiven all my sins. Col. 2:13; Eph. 4:32
God is stern and demanding.	God is accepting and filled with joy and love. Rom. 15:7: Zeph. 3:17
God is passive and cold.	God is warm and affectionate. Is. 40:11: Hos. 11:3-4
God is absent or too busy for me.	God is always with me, He is in me and eager to be with me. Heb. 13:5; I Cor. 3:16; Jer. 31:20; Ez. 34:11-16
God is never satisfied with what I do; God is impatient and angry with me.	God is patient and slow to anger - Exodus 34:6; 2 Pet. 3:9 He has made me accepted, righteous and perfect in Him. Eph. 1:6: Heb. 4:10; II Cor. 5:21
God is mean, cruel or abusive.	God is loving, gentle and protective of me – Jer. 31:3; Is. 42:3; Ps. 18:2

False Belief About God	Truth
God is trying to take all the fun out of life.	God is trustworthy and wants to give me a full life: His will is good, perfect and acceptable for me – Lam. 3:22-23; Jn. 10:10; Rom. 12:1-2
God is controlling and/or manipulative.	God is full of grace and mercy, and He gives me freedom to fail. Heb. 4:15-16: Luke 15:11-16
God is condemning and unforgiving.	He is tender hearted and forgiving; having forgiven all my sins. His heart and arms are always open to me. Ps. 130:1-4; Luke 15:17-24; Col 2:13
God is nit-picking, exacting or a perfectionistic.	God is committed to my growth and proud of me as His growing child. Rom. 8:28-29; Heb. 12:5-11; 2 Cor. 7:14 - He has made me perfect in Him. Heb. 10:4 - It is not by works that he accepts me.
God is punishing me for not pleasing Him. That is the reason I am having pain.	Christ has already been punished for our sins on the cross once and for all. God disciplines those He loves which is different from punishment. Jn. 10:30; 1 Pet. 2:24; Heb. 12:6

Your homework for this chapter will be to put a checkmark by each statement in these lists that represents truth in your life. Some of them will be blatantly obvious and some of them will require some deep thought to see if it is an active lie living as truth in your life. Once you identify your top 5, write down each one along with the opposing truth on a 3x5 card. Carry the cards with you every day in your pocket. Every time you feel your big lie rearing its ugly head you can pull out the card and remember what the truth is.

Remember, the truth may be hard to swallow at first because you have had so many years believing and living the lie. But time, repetition and help from your mentor or small group will bring the truth to the forefront. There is something very powerful and freeing about living in the truth. It is like a massive weight being lifted off of your shoulders. The more of it that you experience the easier it will become to recognize the lies that present themselves throughout the day. The book of John leaves us with a statement about the power of the truth. *And you will know the truth, and the truth will set you free.*

Freedom from everything that keeps our lives, minds and bodies in turmoil and conflict is available. All we have to do is to let go of the truth we think we know as fact and let God speak His truth into our lives.

Chapter 21

Redemption

Chance Encounter – Or is it?

The next morning, after my gauntlet had been thrown down to the almighty, I went to work as usual. I was completely unaware of the plan that had been set in motion as a direct answer to my bold ultimatum. The day passed as any normal day. I really had no thought for the feelings I had been having the day before. As usual they had dissipated into muted shades of gray. I left work early and headed to the grocery store to get a few items for the evening's dinner. I don't remember what I was buying or even what we were going to have for dinner that night. But I will never forget wondering what the look on my face was when God walked around the corner of the end cap and started walking straight towards me down aisle number 7. That's right – God came to meet me – in the grocery store – in aisle number 7!

His name was Kevin. He was a pastor of a small local church and I had known him since I was about 12 years old. He had been an assistant pastor for my dad at the church and also our youth pastor. I had heard stories about him leaving the church and how evil he was because his standards had fallen. I did not know it then but he had found the path to God's grace and was no longer under the law. His peace shone brightly in his eyes as he approached me. As I think back now about who God sent to make first contact with me, there really weren't many people he could have sent that would have had any kind of impact on me. Most anyone that went to any church I hated with a deep hatred that most would reserve for serial killers and people who hurt children. After all, they were the ones who told me and my wife that it was our sin that caused our daughter to be sick. "If you only repented enough or pleased God enough or had enough faith she would get better." I imagined myself grabbing any one of them by the throat and pummeling them senseless. No one was allowed to talk about God around me unless they wanted to be made fun of for being a weak and senseless idiot.

But I knew Kevin was different. I have always prided myself on being able to read people and their character. His was impeccable. Most preachers I knew seemed like they were salesmen always looking for their next victim to sell their load of crap to at a bargain price. Kevin's eyes were honest and calm and he had an aura of complete peace. It was very unnerving to see him walking towards me as the face of God who I had called out the night before. I was completely terror stricken! I was a top salesman in real estate with ice water in my veins and I was scared to death!

As we approached each other and exchanged pleasantries I wondered if he saw the look of terror and confusion that I was attempting to hide. I knew that something was different about this man and I wanted to know more but I surely wasn't about to ask. Could he possibly know what I was thinking? "I just called You out last night!"

After finishing a brief catching up on what each of us had been doing for the past few years he asked me a question that made me shudder. "How about we go to lunch sometime?" "Not a chance in hell" I thought to myself. I was completely freaked out. I told him I would call him but had no idea if I really would. And then we parted ways. I breathed a sigh of relief as he walked away. Was that it? Was that all God had to offer? If so, I had almost breezed right through it. But I was very intrigued by this man and his showing up the day after I laid out my challenge to the Almighty... Almighty indeed. I've been down here getting my ass kicked my whole life and now several thousand people get killed in New York and I've never seen Him. He's not gonna show. This was surely just a fluke... a mere coincidence. But as I went home the thought of this man would not leave my mind. Maybe he had a message for me. Just maybe there might be hope in this world?

Hope... now that was I word that I had never believed in. The only person I was ever able to trust or believe in was myself and my own ability to create something with my own two hands. I pulled myself up and out from a childhood in hell and made something of myself. Don't you ever come in to my office whining and crying about how someone hurt your feelings or made you sad! Didn't you hear me? I said I grew up in hell and I still got up, got dressed and went to work every day, picked myself up by my bootstraps and made something of myself! Hope.... there was no hope. It was just another day on this God forsaken planet. Life's a bitch and then you die.

My favorite song was from Meatloaf's Bat Out of Hell CD. Life is a lemon and I want my money back. I often cranked that song as loud as it would go and screamed it at the top of my lungs. "What about your job? It's defective! What about your childhood? It's defective! What about your feelings? Their defective! What about your friends? Their defective! Life is a lemon and I want my money back!! I know to scream a song is kind of like shouting at the wind. It really isn't going to accomplish a lot but gosh it sure feels good to let it out. Get's the blood flowing and awakens the rage from deep inside. But as usual, my friend indifference comes to bring me back to nothingness.

I went to work the next day with thoughts of my "chance encounter" with Kevin swimming through my mind. As usual it was so hard to turn off my mind once it got started. They called it Hyperfocus Disorder but I wouldn't even learn about that for another ten years. I just knew that once I got started thinking about something, that was all I could think about until there was some sort of conclusion to the matter. I could start playing a video game that had a quest to complete and once that goal was in my mind I couldn't put it down. I would start playing at 10pm and not even know how long I had been playing until I saw the sun coming up. Even sleep took a back seat to the necessary completion of a process in my mind.

Try as I might that day I could not let it go. And then I experienced the second "coincidence" in as many days. I had sold a family a home down past the rock quarry off of Lee Road and I was headed there for an inspection. As I turned down the road I noticed a small church on the corner with the usual marquis in front. I always looked at these to see what stupidity the church was spouting today. They all thought they were so clever with their quips and quotes about how we could just walk in their church or pray a simple prayer and God would just magically show up and everything in your life would be wonderful.

The name on the sign said Baptist Church, and underneath were the words that sent my mind reeling.... Pastor Kevin. Two days in a row!! How was this even possible? It really wasn't. I knew the odds and studied them often. Probabilities and statistics were my gig. You have to know when you get into something if you have good odds of getting a return or not. Coincidence was becoming less and less likely.

I drove past and went to my appointment knowing that this had to be destiny. Maybe this man had a message for me from God. Well if the Almighty had a message for me I surely was not going to miss out on it, so on my way back by I pulled into the parking lot and stopped. There were three cars in the parking lot so I pulled along- side, parked, and went inside. The church itself was very traditional in nature and smelled like a church. I can't really describe the smell but having gone from church to church with dad as he preached hellfire and damnation instantly brought back the memory of that smell.

As I walked in I could hear Kevin talking. I walked the few steps to the first corner and turned to see that his office door was open and someone else was in a chair across from him. I immediately apologized for interrupting and told him that I had been in the area and was just stopping by to say hey. Now for anyone who is not from Georgia, 'hey' is the proper way to greet someone and is similar in meaning and use to 'hello'. I guess it's kind of like 'howdy' in Texas. He seemed to be caught off guard and the person in the chair looked to have just been sharing a problem and appeared to have been crying. I quickly backed out and told him I would stop by later. He asked for my card so he could call me and I lied and said I didn't have any on me. I was a salesman without a phone number, how ironic. I really had no intention of stopping by later. I did not like the experience of walking back into a church and felt everything inside of me telling me to run as far away as I could from whatever I was trying to find out. And so I ran away. I went back to what I knew and what felt safe. I went back to work.

But as it would turn out, my sanctuary of work would betray me. Kevin knew that the events of the last two days had happened for a reason. As he would explain to me several years later, God told him that I needed his help. If he would have told me this up front I most likely would have called him an idiot and run away. I could never fathom at this point that God actually talked to people. But Kevin was a patient man that looked for God to lead, guide and direct in his life.

Kevin knew I was in real estate from our previous conversation and went on a mission to track me down. And track me down he did. The next day, just before lunch he walked into my office and instantly I knew beyond anything about life that I had ever understood – that this man had a message for me from

God! He asked me to lunch and I accepted.

We did eat lunch that day but the food didn't really matter. I didn't tell him about my provocation of God and his showing up. I shared with him my feelings and questions about the church, life in general, and God. These were three very separate topics but all seeming to have a connecting thread and possibly the same answers. Kevin listened keenly and intently, his patient and honest demeanor showing deeply through his eyes and posture. I kept waiting for him to jump in and give me all the answers to all the questions I was throwing at him. I poured it all on him. My anger and rage over my daughter flowed out of my mouth like lava from the mouth of a volcano. At this point it seemed we spent half of our time with her at the hospital. She was having several hundred seizures a day and every medication we tried made it worse. One medication caused her to go into a status seizure that lasted for over two hours.

Her diagnosis was Lennox-Gastaut Syndrome which was classified under Secondary Generalized Epilepsy. In short, it means she has seizures in all four areas of her brain both separately and simultaneously. I was tired of being in the hospital and watching her suffer all of the time. How could there be a God that would do this to my child?

Kevin must have listened to me rant for over 2 hours with no real insight into my life until he finally started asking questions. There is a Proverb that says "Questions provoke thought but accusations stir up anger." That may make sense for some people but his questions were just plain pissing me off. Questions I had – I wanted answers! There was no shortage of questions in my head. "If there is a God why would he let all those people die? Why do bad things happen to good people? Where was he when I was a child? Was he the one who hurt my little girl just to punish me?"

Some people say that it isn't polite to answer a question with a question. But it seems that a question has the ability to send the mind in a specific direction that causes a person to answer their own question. And when you answer a question yourself it makes the answer your own. This was definitely a different approach than I remembered from my past. In my past it always seemed everyone was telling me what to believe and never letting me ask any questions. And if I did have a question I was labeled rebellious or someone who didn't have enough faith.

"Why are Christians such self-righteous, judgmental, better-than-thou !#%&!?" I am sick and tired of seeing them look down on me like I'm less of a person because I don't go to church. Kevin tried to explain that all Christians were not that way and even talked about how this all began as early as the first century. He said that there have always been people that use the name of God and Christianity for their own purpose and gain. Take a look at the Crusades. People have been killing each other for centuries all in the name of God. Even when the Apostle Paul told the story of Christ to King Agrippa the affect of self serving Christians had already begun to be felt. King Agrippa told Paul that the story of Christ sounded very compelling and that he would consider becoming a Christian were it not for Christians. What a condemning statement for an entire group of people whose leader loved them enough to die for them.

I left our meeting that day probably more perplexed than before we talked. But God was not going to give up on me and neither was Kevin. He knew that there was purpose in our lives running into each other. We continued to have lunch about twice a week for the next six months. I began to look forward to our lunches and would even write down my questions for him. Each question was usually met with more questions and the suggestion of a book to read. Of course anyone who knew Kevin or had seen his library and massive collection of books would know that you couldn't leave his presence without having him suggest something of value to read. I really admired that about Kevin. He seemed to have the uncanny ability to listen to anything you were saying and suggest the perfect book to push you and your thinking in the right direction.

Kevin seemed to take great joy in spending time with me walking through my life. I think he found purpose in helping someone who was lost find their way. I found it easy to listen to him and began to appreciate the way that he helped me to reach my own answer instead of being spoon fed the standard religious clichés.

The next day as promised Kevin brought me a book that he had mentioned in our lunch conversation. The book was called Wisdom Hunter by Randall Arthur. He said it would help me see another side to Christianity. Now I had never really read a book about God before and novels were for girls so I took the book home and just stared at it. All I ever read about was business, marketing and psychology so do I really want to open this door? But once I became intrigued the battle was over and I was off and reading.

The story told of an overbearing, pious, judgmental preacher, much like my father, that lost everything he held dear over the course of a few days. This great loss caused him to question everything he thought he knew as fact about God and began his search for something new. It was a search for something that cannot easily be defined into a set of rules with which to judge by.

I greatly identified with the sadness that was experienced throughout the book but more importantly saw something I had never seen before. This writer was depicting a God that had great love for his children no matter what they did. It showed a group of believers that shared this love freely with anyone they came in contact with. Could this be I wondered? Are there actually Christians that not only like each other but even love everyone? Now this I had to check out. And so the next Sunday I did the unthinkable. I needed to know if a world like this actually existed. I needed to know if God actually existed. And so I woke up early, got the family ready and walked into the doors of Kevin's church.

Your homework for this chapter is to identify where you run to when you get into a position that feels uncomfortable. Just like I had the urge to run back to work as soon as I smelled that church for the first time in years, you too can identify what it is that you're running from. What is it that you are scared of confronting and what do you use as a coping mechanism to keep you from ever facing it? It may be time to come face to face with the answer to both of these questions and finally force yourself to face whatever it is that makes you uncomfortable.

Chapter 22
Redemption and Revelation
Conversion of a Skeptic

It really is amazing how once you ask God to reveal himself to you how he actually starts to show up everywhere. You may not see him at first and you may wonder why certain things are happening the way that they are. But it really is exciting when you turn around and look at the work in progress and see His gentle affirming brushstrokes on the canvas.

I began attending Kevin's church every Sunday and meeting with him once or twice a week for lunch. The church was small and the people seemed very genuine in their desire to be kind to other people. Having Kevin to disciple me on a weekly basis was invaluable. Discipleship really is a lost art. Most people that I have worked for or with have taught me things so that I could help them in some way. Kevin never asked for anything in return. I kept waiting for the other half of the timeshare shoe to drop but it never did.

After about 4 months of reading books and asking question after question, I finally decided to place my trust in someone I could not see. I didn't pray a prayer or have any special kind of ceremony. I just told God that I believed in Him and that I wanted Him to show me more of who he was no matter the cost. I remember having lunch with Kevin and telling him that "I think I've crossed over. I think I'm one of them Christians." The word was painful to say because of all the pain in my life caused by Christianity. He smiled and laughed as he assured me that I didn't have to call myself by that name. He said I could be a follower of Jesus Christ. I liked the sound of that. I wish more Christians would follow the self-less, loving nature of the man they claim to follow.

Strap your seatbelts on and put your tray tables in their locked position because the ride is about to derail! This was my step onto a path less traveled and I didn't go down the path half hearted. I was running at full speed ahead. I was on a mission to make up for all the wrongs that I had done and that had been done to me. My first step was to start donating some time to working with the teenagers at the church. I started visiting people in the hospital. Everywhere I went I was telling everyone about my new God. Of course, I knew all of the Bible stories from growing up but their interpretation was all wrong. Kevin walked with me through story after story as we studied the Bible. I was on a mission to figure out who God was. My biggest mistake at this point was my belief that the work of God in my life was done. I believed in Him as my Savior and now I just had to help other people to do the same. I became hyper-focused on defining God and making sure everyone else knew what my definitions of God were. I was very brash and always felt that because I had studied it that my conclusions were from God. Now this is a very dangerous spot to be living because when you believe something is from God you become completely justified in your actions. I can tell someone off and because I believe it came from God I am justified. I am in a sense God's messenger.

And then, once we have God figured out we say things like He is the same yesterday, today, and forever but then we are the ones who have determined what His sameness is. What if one of is traits is that He is always different based on who He needs to be to us so that He can bring us back to Him. That would mean that one of His traits that is always the same, is that He is always communicating to us in different ways. Try chewing on that one for a while. Why not let God be the Almighty and stop trying to define Him and let Him define Himself to us. In defining Himself he said only that "I Am." That's pretty broad isn't it? I am assuming that I Am covers... well... everything! The problem is that He cannot define Himself if we are doing it for Him. He will be inside whatever box you create for Him. Stop building a box for God and start building a double quadropolydecahedrenagon. I don't know what that is but it sounds complex with a lot of layers, levels and sides to it that can never be figured out. Let Him be the mysterious God that He wants to be and then He can start to show you who He is and who you are in relationship to Him. He will reveal the layers, levels and sides that you need to see as you are ready to see them.

I was moving so fast that the wheels were barely staying on the tracks. I began spending more time working with the youth and less time working my job. I figured that because I was doing good things that I could spend my time doing "God's work" instead of working to make money. I thought at the time that my logic was sound. But at the same time that I thought I had it all figured out, God was working his plan.

Are you building a box in which to keep your idea of God? Spend some time in your journal tonight. Ask God to reveal to you some of the limits that you have put on Him. I remember sitting in a session and telling the counselor that there is no way for me to replace my childhood. It is lost and gone and I will never be able to know what it feels like to be nurtured. The counselor asked me if I believed that God did not have the capacity to enter my heart, mind and soul and give me the feeling of nurturing. I instantly realized that I had placed a limit on what God could do in this area of my life because of my belief that I could never get that feeling back. I closed my eyes, gave God permission to do what only He could do and then sat back to enjoy the ride. His hands reached into my soul and held my heart ever so gently. His spirit enveloped my body in a caress that made me feel like a baby being rocked gently to sleep in the arms of its mother. Memories of my mother taking me to the park for a picnic and pushing me on a swing instantly came rushing into my mind. I was being nurtured! I was being loved as a child needs to be loved! All because I believed that He was all powerful and I believed that He was able.

What does God want to do in your life that you don't really believe is possible? It's time to throw out the box that you have created for God to live in. Spend some time today to write in your journal. Open your heart and your mind and God will guide your pen.

Chapter 23
Redemption
My Path to Brokenness

The next five years is all a blur. My only goals became my search to define who God was while at the same time doing good whenever I could in an attempt to please God and make up for my past. This five year time span I like to call my intellectual search for God. I read the Bible over and over, I read books, wrote journals to define who I thought God was based on what I read, and I preached what I learned to anyone that would listen. But I was on a journey to define God and not to experience Him. It really is funny how closed minded we can be when we are on such a journey. People can attempt to tell us the way that we are headed and that we are only seeing one side of God but because of our extreme distrust we rely only on what we see and feel. The emotions that we feel throughout the process seem to represent truth because we have not yet learned how to manage our emotions or have a core truth to believe in.

Things in my life seemed to be spiraling out of control. And now we remember that I asked God to show me who he was – at any cost. A bold request to say the least. At any cost means that I give Him complete control to do what He needs to do in my life to cleanse, purify and reveal to me who He is and who I am.

Over the next few years my wife and I experienced the real estate crash of the mid to late 2000's. I tried everything to try to make the money keep flowing in but no matter what I did, it ended in failure. For the first time in my life I couldn't make anything happen in business. It was like all of my magic mojo was gone and there was nothing I could do about it. I remember the story of how God took proud and haughty King Nebuchadnezzar and reduced him to a beast in the field. I felt exactly the same way. I spiraled down into depression as we neared the bottom of our bank account. I kept spending more and more time serving God in church without getting paid thinking that this was certainly the answer for my troubles.

Every day things between my wife and I got more tense and more strained. I felt that she was holding me personally responsible for the real estate crash. I thought back to how frivolous we had been with the money we had made over the years and wished that I had been more of a saver instead of a spender.

The spiritual warfare in my mind was so intense I couldn't sleep at night. I tossed and turned and went long periods of time sleeping only 2 or 3 hours a night. The tormentor would come at night and keep me awake as he condemned me over and over for the things from my past. My dreams became so violent that I didn't want to go to sleep. The battle for my soul was raging and I had no idea if I was going to survive or that the battle was even happening. I just thought that I was going crazy. Things began to fall apart in the churches that I worked in as I was pushing harder and harder trying to make sure that everyone else lived up to the standard of righteousness that I felt had to be maintained.

I started seeing a psychiatrist because I truly did believe that I was going crazy. My dreams were escalating as visions of the fear from my childhood tried to poke their way through. I would find myself running through a fog being chased by something evil that I could not see – but I knew it was after me. One night I even cracked two ribs in my sleep as I dove off the end of my bed trying to get away from the evil attacking me in my mind.

The condemning voice of the accuser in my head raged so loud that I could not find a peaceful moment anywhere. "You'll never amount to anything. Just quit and go back to the way you were. How stupid and weak do you have to be to believe in something you can't see. You're strong and you don't need a God. And just look at everything He's done to your business. He took your house. He took your cars. He doesn't love you. Let's just quit and everything will be ok."

The first shrink I talked to wanted to medicate me. I had seen people on medication in the past and so I refused. I didn't want to be a drooling zombie as I tried to work hard to dig out of the hole that we were in. The second and third shrinks were no help either. They just tried to give me solutions to combat the symptoms that I was experiencing. No one could tell me why I was hearing what I was hearing in my head. I began to think that I was losing my mind.

At this point I decided to take a break from God. I had been serving Him tirelessly for several years now in spite of my failing businesses, in spite of my strained relationships and in spite of several church situations that left me and my wife emotionally damaged. And so I found another business opportunity and moved to the other side of town to get away from everything that reminded me of my past and looked to start over from scratch. The funny part about being so driven is that when things go wrong you just work harder and find more ways to make it work on your own. If God's not going to fix it then I will.

And so I pushed into the new business opportunity and ignored God for a while. And that's when it happened. Once I was out of the way and gave up control of how I was going to live my life for God, He was able to step in and begin his work. I stayed out of church for almost a year and listened to all of my 'Job like' friends give me reasons for why I had failed. I heard them belittle me for losing faith and for not going to church. But I didn't care anymore. I had tried everything I could try to figure God out, and I had failed. I had served and given my time and hadn't gotten anything in return. I had been on an intellectual search to define God and had failed miserably. This was my point of true brokenness. I had tried to manufacture happiness, peace, success and contentment and I had failed. I had tried everything I knew how to try and I was left wanting more. There was a hole in my soul that I had tried to fill with sex, love, friends, religion, work, hobbies, and a host of other devices and the hole was still there. Absolutely nothing had worked. That burning feeling that there is something more was stronger than ever. "Please help me God." I prayed. "I have tried to do all of this on my own and I can't do it anymore. Would you please come do it for me?"

What are you still in control of? What area of your life do you still manipulate and manufacture? Until you resign your control of those areas God will not be able to complete His work. Sounds like a homework assignment.

Chapter 24
Revelation

I Love a Good Promise

Jeremiah 29:11 *"For I know the plans I have for you, plans to prosper you and not to harm you, plans to give you hope and a future"*

What's not to love? Everyone loves a good promise. Especially a promise like this one filled with prosperity and protection. But how many times do you hear someone quoting Paul or Christ asking us to share in His suffering? Not many I assure you. But many of us have suffered and we wonder the meaning of that suffering and why we had to endure it. We finished the last chapter with talking about resigning control of certain areas to allow God to do his work. Jeremiah chapter 29 can actually help us facilitate this. It can help us transition from what we know in our heads to make sure that we are attempting to feel it in our hearts. How many people do you know that you would consider a 'head knowledge' Christian as opposed to a 'heart knowledge' Christian? If you've never used your heart before that's ok. We are going to be talking about how God can help you to activate your heart to feel His presence.

The opposite can also exist where God is just a bunch of feelings and the truth is never introduced. John mentions in the

Bible that Christ was full of grace and truth. Not a balance of each, but a completely full measure of both. Christians have fought back and forth for years on whether grace and acceptance should be shown to sinners or if we should stand on the street corner with a bullhorn telling them all that they are going to hell. I think that Jeremiah can help us understand where I went wrong in my intellectual search for God and where many Christians are struggling as they serve in churches in an attempt to try to find their identity in Christ. It is so easy to get bogged down with doing religious things that we may miss the fact that all that we are really asked to do is to surrender and waive the white flag. Once we waive the flag we can then allow Christ to heighten our awareness to the work that was already done. So let's dig into what I like to call the 'Jeremiah 29:11 enlightenment.'

God says, *"For I know the plans I have for you, plans to prosper you and not to harm you, plans to give you hope and a future"*
Now this all sounds fantastic and this is where most people stop. Put it on the fridge or on a bumper sticker and I will take it all day long and twice on Sunday. But the passage doesn't stop here. It continues with verse 12. *Then you will call on me and come and pray to me, and I will listen to you.*

Remember my prayer from the end of the last chapter? "Please help me God. I have tried to do all of this on my own and I can't do it anymore. Would you please come do it for me?" Then you will call on me is not me coming to God and telling Him what I am going to do for Him. It is me on my face, completely broken at His feet, asking Him to do what I am incapable of doing. I initially came to God with my head and told Him what I would now be doing for Him. After all, He was really lucky to get a go getter like me working for Him for the furthering of His kingdom. What a find He had gotten when I was converted. I was still in control even though I would have told you or anyone else that I was completely surrendered to God. That really is the funny thing about control and surrender. You don't know that you have it or are not in it until it is revealed to you.

Now to me, verses 12 and 13 are a significantly greater promise than verse 11 because He tells me that if I call on Him in this capacity that He will listen to me. How many times do you hear someone say that God is silent in their life right now? It is my contention that God is never silent. I believe that He is always speaking but that we either have so much pain and anger screaming in our mind that we can't hear Him or that we won't stop talking long enough for Him to speak. You know the type of person I am talking about. They sit across from you at lunch and tell you about their life and all of the people that bother them and that they can't stand? And every time you try to interject with a helpful thought or question they just begin with another story about their life. This person cannot hear anything because they never stop talking.

Now let's look at the last part of the promise. *"You will seek me and find me when you seek me with all your heart."* Notice that it does not say that you will find me when you have me completely figured out. Figuring it all out is head knowledge and when we have it all figured out then faith and trust are not necessary. This passage says that you will find me when you seek me with all your heart. So how do you seek God with all your heart instead of with your mind? The answer to this will be different for each person. Your path to God and the perfect peace that he freely offers is between you and God and only He can lead you down that path. You can have a mentor, counselor or small group in the process to help guide you along the way, but the majority of the work will be done as God reveals to you the areas in which you are in control and you lay down at His feet each area one at a time and say "I cannot do this alone. I need you!"

I remember when I reached this specific point in my journey. When I was confronted with the choice to keep learning more about God or to completely change gears and see if I could actually feel God and experience Him. Ask God if it's your time to go to the next step. To move from knowing Him in your head to feeling Him in your heart. Once you are feeling Him in your heart you can move to hearing Him and seeing Him work in your life every minute of every day. To live the relationship that He originally intended for Adam and Eve. Is it your time? Ask Him? He will let you know.

Chapter 25
Redemption
Simply Grace – Nothing More

After my heartfelt prayer to God I felt a sense of resignation to my life. I had raised the white flag in my search to define and serve God in my power. I was tired of trying to manufacture how I wanted to feel based on my performance in life. I was beginning to realize that I had taken the same principles that I had learned about religion growing up and applied them to my new Christian walk. How many times do I have to keep making that mistake before I realize that the things I learned in the past are not necessarily true? Apparently quite a few.

Now that I was out of the way God had a chance to come into my life and play. I was now living on the North side of town in Atlanta and everywhere I went people would ask me if I had been to Northpoint Church. It was almost like everyone in the entire town went to church there or that God was putting someone in my path every day that would invite me to this same church. I felt God giving me a feeling of peace that it was ok to go ahead and get reconnected to a church and so I started attending Northpoint Church.

It was a really nice feeling to attend a larger church and get lost in the crowd so to speak. No one knew who I was, I could sit in the back and be anonymous, no one would ask me to be their youth pastor and I could just be fed for a period of time as I looked for healing to take place. It wasn't long until we decided to get involved in a small group to look for some connectedness with other couples in the church. I had led many small groups in the past but felt compelled not to lead this time. I felt I was being asked to take a back seat. Without really knowing it I was starting to hear and see the leading of the Holy Spirit as He led me to feel at peace with certain decisions that were outside the norm of what I usually did. In the past I had to be in charge of everything because I always felt that I could do everything better than everyone else. Heck, I couldn't even go to a PTA meeting without wanting to fire everyone and reorganize their corporate structure! But I was letting go and seeing if God could do a better job with this next phase of my life than I had done with the previous one. What did I have to lose? The last few phases of my life had really sucked!

Once again, when I was out of the way the miraculous hand of God showed up to be able to work. One of the men from the small group was working with young teen boys who had been addicted to drugs and invited me on a retreat to spend some time mentoring these boys. I thought it sounded great and agreed to go along. When I showed up to head out to the place we were camping the van was full and the only seat left was riding with an old Marine named Mike. I was a little bit put out. I came to have fun with the boys and they stick me with this old dude for 3 hours in a truck! I was less than thrilled but as we headed down the road Mike looked across at me and must have known that I needed help. He asked me about my life and I laid it all on him. I never have been shy about sharing my story and am probably an open book that some people would like to close and lock in a drawer somewhere. But Mike listened for about 2 hours and identified with my heart and my struggles. He said he could tell that my heart was in the right place but that I was dealing with identity issues. I had no idea what he was talking about. What are you talking about identity issues for Mike? I know who I am. Or so I thought. I guess it's kind of like the step where we said it will work until it doesn't. We really do think that we know who we are until we realize that we don't.

After the retreat and at the end of our ride back home Mike told me to get in touch with someone at Simply Grace Counseling and he would talk to me about my identity issues. I thanked him and made the call to set up my first appointment.

This was the first step in the series of events that took place for me to begin my change from knowing God in my head to feeling God in my heart. From being mired in a system of laws and behavior in an attempt to earn favor to crossing over into grace, love and total acceptance. As I look back at these events, tears fill my eyes as I think of how God loves me so much that He spent the time to orchestrate all of this just for me. Nothing I can do will make Him love me more or less. All I had to do was get out of the way so He could be God and let Him do the work.

My first appointment was so much different than the shrinks I had seen in the past. My counselors name was Jason and he worked very fast as he went immediately to the heart of the matter. "The voices you are hearing in your head that condemn you are not you." I was lapping it up as fast as he could pour it out. You mean that's not me producing those thoughts? No, that is indwelling sin left in every one of us by Adam and it's only job is to counter the job of the Holy Spirit by telling you who you are not. It tells you that you are a failure and that you will never be a success. It tells you these things so that it can keep you where you are in life. And for those of us who have a bad religious experience we can even believe that at is the voice of God calling to condemn us. I was taking notes at light speed as it was all making so much sense. It was like the lights had been off for so long and they were starting to come on. I was in awe of God for sending me this beautiful message right when I needed it.

Jason gave me a book called Grace Walk by Steve McVey to help me understand the difference between living a life under the law and living a life under grace. I read each week and highlighted passages that peaked my curiosity and brought them in to discuss for our weekly meeting.

In our second session Jason asked me how something made me feel and I told him I didn't know. He handed me a feelings word sheet with a list of feeling words that was 2 pages long. As I looked at the pages I began to search for words that I actually knew what they felt like. I knew how to emulate what a feeling looked like because that's just part of being a good salesman. But out of all of the words on the list I could only circle 6 that I absolutely knew what they felt like. I was stunned to see what I was missing out on, so I asked God to show me what each of these feelings felt like. Maybe I should have thought that request out a little more before I threw it out there. I guess it's kind of like asking God for patience. You better strap yourself in because the only way to test patience is to... well... test your patience! And so the journey of learning to feel began.

Each week we would diagram the events that had happened in the past and the false beliefs and coping mechanisms that had been put into place. Jason would remind me that a coping mechanism may have been necessary as a child to protect me from being hurt in an unsafe situation. But now I had to ask myself if it was safe to remove that wall and let people begin to come closer to me. I started to realize that part of me really wanted people to come close and touch me but that when they started to get too close I would push them away.

At this point I didn't really remember the beatings from dad and blamed all of the crazy childhood on mom. We took a look at the things that had happened in that relationship and started to walk through forgiveness and letting go of the things that I was holding on to. Jason explained that forgiveness is not for the other person. It is for me. He gave me one of my favorite anonymous quotes that says that un-forgiveness is the poison that I drink in hopes that you will die. We went through several forgiveness sessions where we pretended the person was in a chair in front of me and I charged them with everything that they had done to me and then I released them from what I felt they owed me. I was learning that forgiveness was more about the releasing the debt that I felt was owed to me. As long as my parents owed me the debt of another childhood than that debt had to be paid before I could be whole. Since that debt could not be paid the only alternative would be to forgive the debt. Each week we dug a little deeper until we came to the point that God felt I was ready to cross over into grace.

Your homework this week is to diagram an event from your past that needs to be forgiven, under the formula we introduced in an earlier chapter. Event → Feeling → Belief → Coping Mechanism. Write down your event, how it made you feel, what it made you believe and what did you change in your life to keep it from ever happening again.

Chapter 26
Redemption

Crossing Over into Grace

I continued to read each week and go to my weekly session. Jason would ask me why I was progressing so fast. I told him that I believed it was because I wanted to know Christ more than I wanted to breathe. I had lived my entire life for myself looking to get everything I had wanted and I had come up completely bankrupt and lost. I wanted something different and I was no longer going to define what that something different was. I was going to get out of the way and let God do the work this time.

The next week at church was one of the most precious moments that I have ever experienced on this planet. I find tears running down my cheeks as I simply write the account of what took place. On Sunday morning in February of 2007 I crossed over into grace. Now I know that this is a bit of a cryptic statement but crossing over into grace is kind of like that movie The Matrix. When the hero of the movie Neo keeps asking what The Matrix is, his mentor only tells him that no one can be told what the matrix is. You have to experience it for yourself to know what it is. Crossing over into grace is very similar in that the only way you will be able to know how it feels or what it is, will be when it happens for you.

On this Sunday morning Jeff Henderson was teaching a series called Mythbusters. It was about all of the myths that exist in Christianity that we believe as truth and because we believe the lie as truth, we never get to experience the real truth. Jeff had a treadmill on the stage and was sharing it as an analogy for the Christian life. We keep getting on this treadmill and working hard to please God and the church. This treadmill says that the better I am the more God loves me, so we work hard and keep trying to prove that we are worthy of redemption and God's love. We work hard as we hope to make up for all the wrongs in our life. And then we get off of the treadmill and notice that we haven't gotten anywhere. So what do we do? We rededicate ourselves to work harder. Maybe we quit for a time because it's not working or we're just not feeling it and then we rededicate. If I can only run this race just right then everything will come together. This cycle can go on and on for many years. Jeff then challenged everyone to get off the treadmill and just let God love them for who they are. He said that God loves you no matter what and that there is nothing you can do to make God love you more or less. I had heard Jason saying this in therapy sessions but it was just starting to sink in.

And then God used Jeff to hit me right in the center of my heart. The real truth in my case was the belief that there was no way that God could really love me. I had done too much. I had caused too much pain. Too much had been done to me. There's no way that he could take me back or even want me. I was broken and He could love me a little but not like everyone else. As I sat in my seat with these words running through my mind, Jeff spoke directly to those words from the stage. These new words were powerful and in my mind it was as if they were coming directly from the mouth of God to my ears! He said, "Some of you are sitting there and you just said, "Not me Jeff. God can't really love me. I've done too much. Too much has been done to me. God can't really love me like He does everyone else. But He does and all you have to do is accept that love."

It's hard to understand the concept that someone is going to give you something so valuable and that you don't have to do anything for it in return but at that moment it all made sense. He loved me! He loved me, He loved me, He loved me!!! I didn't have to do anything for it! He just loved me in spite of the hurt that had been done to me. He loved me in spite of the hurt I had caused. He didn't care! He just loved me! His love washed over me and began to fill places in my body that I had never felt before. The soft hazel eyes from so many years ago began to fill with tears. For the first time since I was 8 years old tears were flowing from my eyes as they cleansed my soul. My heart was warm and bursting with a feeling I had never experienced as a piece of the hole that was inside me began to fill with something new... Love. I was sitting in church in front of everyone sobbing like a little baby. The tears were warm and felt like a hug. I knew His arms were around me as I felt Him rocking me slowly like his lost love child. The lost son in his father's arms for the first time.

It has been said that you cannot give what you have never received. Because I had never received love like this I could not give it to anyone else. My own son was now 15 years old. I had been trying for quite some time to show him love and accept him for who he was as a young man but had met with difficulty at every turn. Much of my acceptance was based on performance. This very same day that I accepted the love of Christ I hugged my son with a giant bear hug and told him that I loved him. I had never done that in his 15 years of existence on this earth. Until I accepted unconditional love from God I did have it in me to give to anyone else.

If you have not experienced this moment in your life do not attempt to manufacture it. Surrender what you think you want and ask God to set in place your series of circumstances that will lead you to this moment. Recognize your absolutes and release them to God. Be open for anything and He will take you there.

Chapter 27
Redemption
The Damascus Road

Now that I had accepted this amazing love everything felt different. This could have been a moment where I decided that I had gotten what I was looking for and that I had reached my destination. But I was beginning to learn from my past mistakes. I had thought that I knew all of the answers many times before and became complacent and comfortable. Now I was learning to feel the leading of the Holy Spirit and I knew He had more to show me. I remember hearing the story of Enoch who walked with God so much that one day the two of them just kept walking right up into heaven. I figure that until God and I are so close in our walk that we walk into heaven together that there must be further to go. And so I kept going. Although I was not aware at this point there was much more healing that needed to take place and much more revelation from God about who He was and wanted to be in my life.

I was invited by Jason to take a 10 month group class from Grace Ministries called the Advanced Discipleship Training. I was starting to think again that I had it all figured out so Jason told me the class would help me teach other people the message of grace and if I happened to get something from it then it was a bonus. The program began in August of 2007 and was filled with an eclectic group of individuals. Each person had their own story and reason for being there but each was looking for some sort of new enlightenment from God that would somehow make all of the pain and hurt in their lives make sense.

Each week we dug a little deeper into understanding how our past affects our future and how we can let the beliefs that we internalized from the events in our past control us. As we dug in I began to realize how emotionally disconnected that I still was and that maybe I needed to go deeper into my childhood to find a sense of how to reconnect emotionally with God and other people. To not only see them as bodies but to be able to feel them and share in their lives.

One of the mentors in the group was named Jimmy and every week he was challenging me to go deeper. One night in an attempt to help me connect to my emotions he asked me to close my eyes and look deep into my childhood. The class got quiet and they all shared in the moment that we were experiencing. After about 10 seconds I began to see through the fog from my dreams and the urge to run was overwhelming. I became sick to my stomach and felt the urge to vomit and pass out. I ran from the class with the feeling that I wanted to keep running and never come back. Whatever was buried here was buried for a reason and did not need to be dug up.

I waited outside for a while knowing that I could not leave. I had been running my whole life and it was time to stop running. I knew that God had something for me to see and I was determined to see it. Of course it wasn't long until Jimmy came out and sat down with me. He asked me if I had considered giving God permission to let me feel what He wanted me to feel. I thought this was an interesting idea. Could this be the same as accepting love? Could it be as easy as stepping out of the way, letting down my guard and giving Him permission to let me feel what He wanted me to feel? Most of my search up to this point had been to look for the feelings that I wanted.

I went home that night and went to my office and stared at my computer screen. I opened up a blank page for a journal, got down on my knees and gave God permission to let me feel what He wanted me to feel. I sat there for an hour and nothing happened so I went to bed. And once again God was faithful to his promise.

Have you ever had one of those moments that is almost indescribable? A moment that you just can't explain to many people without them looking at you a little funny as you can tell they are thinking, "Are you serious" or "Have you lost your mind?" I kind of imagine that is what it must have been like for Paul on the road to Damascus. Can you imagine him trying to tell his friends that he saw a living Christ in a bright white light? Sure Paul. Can someone please check his flask to see what he's been drinking? A little less wine for Paul everyone. Well this is my Damascus road moment.

As I laid down in bed that night and got comfortable... I heard the voice of God for the first time ever. It wasn't audible. It was more of an internal voice asking a question that I knew was not of myself. How did I know that the question wasn't from me? Because it was a ridiculous, off the wall, way out in left field kind of a question that made me sit up in bed and say out loud, "What the hell are you talking about!?!?!" I mean, you have my entire life to show up and help me out and this is the first time you show up and this is what you ask me??? It reminded me of when Job heard the voice of God after 36 chapters of suffering. Was this finally my Job moment?

What was the question that dug so deep and rattled me down to the core? As I laid there quietly in bed I heard the question, "What is your favorite color?" Really, that's what you ask? What the hell are you talking about? He asked again and this time he said my name. "Brian, what is your favorite color?" I knew that this was a big moment for me so I paused and thought for a short moment. And then as I slowly began to figure it out, I began to cry. I don't have one Father. I don't have a favorite color. At that same moment I realized what He was really asking me. Color in life is a metaphor for feeling. We use it to describe how we feel. I can feel red with rage or just be a little blue. I can feel the warmth of orange or the dismal nature of gray. To decide not have a favorite color was a choice not to feel. It was a choice to be indifferent. I instantly heard a phrase rolling through my mind. "A young man looks for what is missing. He looks with all his might. What is your favorite color, God asks on a cold, dark, dreary night." Now I have never written a poem before so I knew instantly that this was a message from God's heart directly to mine.

So I went back to my computer and cried for the next 2 hours as God wrote from His heart to mine the story of a small boy still locked deep down inside a cold dark castle that was constructed many years ago. The castle was constructed with such haste that no doors were built for enter or exit. And the small boy was still locked inside with no color, no emotion, and no feeling.

I Don't Have a Favorite Color

A young man looks for what is missing
He looks with all his might
What is your favorite color, God asks
On a cold, dark, dreary night

I don't have a favorite color
It wasn't allowed you see
To have a favorite color
Would require individuality

Toe the line and walk the course
Was the agenda of the day
Don't step outside of the line
Or there would be hell to pay

Do not think and do not question
Never ever ask why
Why don't I have a favorite color
They took it with a lie

They said I was bad and I must be punished
As they put me in my place
It was a system built on guilt and shame
And shame eventually won the race

I remember liking blue
And sometimes even red
I'd long for these strong, bold colors
As I laid crying under my bed

Why did they choose to hurt me
Was it to put their minds at ease
Or did they not know how to love a child
And teach him to have peace

Why did they have such anger
Why didn't they want me to live
Why did they take my colors
To have them back, anything I would give

Why not orange or yellow
These soft and warm autumn tones
They seem to feel like a warm embrace
Or a hug that goes deep into my bones

196

Why didn't I get the warmth
Or the hug from mom and dad
Why did they choose to hate me
And teach me that I was bad

Maybe it should be pink or purple
Colors so royal and sweet
Oh to feel like a king just once
Instead of a hand, a soft, loving kiss my cheek would meet

The pain is hidden by walls
Walls that you cannot get past
These walls are black and ugly
It seems they are built to last

But maybe God has another plan
I see some pink shining through
His soft lips yearning to kiss my cheek
And the walls are turning to shades of blue

How do I find what has been lost, if I even can
How do I feel the pain locked up in these walls
"Suck it up you little pansy ass
And take it like a man"

How do I feel the hurt and pain
Of a small 8 year old boy
Whose pain was used to turn him into
A man that doesn't know how to feel, And may never know true
joy

A man whose only color is gray
Because he will never ever take sides

He will choose to see neither good nor bad
For in that, no disappointment lies

Never be happy, never be sad
Expect everyone to fail you
If you expect to see the worst in the end
You're not surprised when it comes true

This is the key to the bricks in the wall
I must find a color other than gray
To make a choice to feel again
And give God a chance to play

Come play with me God, come play with my heart
I give my walls to you
Flood my soul with your love
And teach me something new

Yellow or Orange, Blue or Red
It does not matter to me
Show me my favorite color
And I'll find the 8 year old broken, hurt child
Locked up somewhere deep inside of me.

_bc_

This moment marks the first time in my life that I came to terms with the fact that what I experienced as a child was not normal and allowed myself to remember. To purposely bring something that had been buried under the fog of war to come to light. There is something very freeing about the light. Consider the child locked in that deep dark pit of despair longing to see the light of day. The loneliness he or she must feel and the longing to be let out to play if even for a minute or two. But our busy schedule and unwillingness to feel any pain will keep us from letting that child out. I remember the first time in therapy that I was given the homework of asking the child version of myself what he would tell the adult version. As I sat down that night with my journal open and my eyes closed, I began to cry as I realized what little 8 year old Brian wanted to say to me. "Tell big Brian that it's ok now. Tell him that I think it's safe to let me come out and play. Tell him that it's ok to stop protecting me. I really would love to feel what it's like to play again." At that moment I realized why I was so hard on my son. Everything was business because that was all that I knew. I realized that as an adult I didn't know what it was like to play. I made the decision that day to let little Brian out to have some fun. Even if I had to find a sledgehammer to create a door into that castle, I was going to let him come out to play.

What message does God have for you? He has a Damascus road moment waiting for each and every one of us. Don't be complacent where you are. Don't settle for just good enough. Give God permission to take you anywhere He wants to take you and remove from your mind any expectation of what it should be. His work is more powerful and beautiful than you can imagine and you can trust that He will hold you tightly in His arms no matter where He decides to take you. It's an incredible feeling! If you are willing – He is able.

Your homework for this chapter is to see if the younger version of yourself has a message for you. Get somewhere quiet and dig in. If you need support from a friend or even from a counselor then ask for help.

Chapter 28
Redemption and Revelation
Out of the Gray

Now that I had discovered that I didn't have a favorite color I began to wonder what my color might be. My usual instincts would be to run straight into that problem with guns a blazing and make sure I determined what it was. But not this time. I was starting to learn that the work that God could do was far easier and more powerful than the work that I could do. And so I surrendered to him my wants and rights that I thought I had to have a favorite color.

It is really interesting as we take a look at how quickly something we want can follow the progression of turning from a want into a need. It may start as something we see that is desirable and then we may notice that someone else has what we want. And we really like it and think it would make our life easier so it moves from want status to need status. Once we need it the desire for it grows until it graduates to a right. I deserve it. I've worked hard my whole life and that person has one and they don't ever do anything. It's just not fair! Fair, now there's a word that is misused on a daily basis. Someone who doesn't get the latest thingamajig that they need so desperately says it isn't fair. Why not try being a child who goes to bed without dinner because their parents are addicts. Now that's not fair.

I continued going to my weekly class, reading and doing my homework. Each week at the class was a great checkpoint from my chaotic week to remind me where I was going. It really is easy throughout the week to fall back into taking control. One of my counselors named George gave me a great way to look at the ways that we go back and forth from letting the flesh lash out with anger or frustration and from allowing the Spirit to shine through. He said that the initial goal cannot be to be in the Spirit all of the time because failure is just around the corner. Remember that we have lived the old way for so many years that it is the norm and we have to train our minds to think and live a different way. The goal has to be to notice as soon as possible that we are acting out in the flesh instead of in the spirit. The flesh will come and attempt to take over as things happen that push our buttons and make us question who we are. Many times we can go days, weeks, or even months being in a selfish fleshly pattern and not even realize it. What if you could notice the flesh pattern you are in within 2 days? What if as you grow in the Holy Spirit you were able to shorten it even further to 2 hours, 2 minutes, or even 2 seconds? Think of the mind as a muscle, and just like any muscle it gets stronger with practice. The more you practice being in the Spirit the more you will notice when you are stressed, frustrated, angry and slipping out of the Spirit.

George also shared another great analogy with me. If I came to you and asked you if I could drive your car, you would consider how well you know me, think about my track record with you and then if you thought I was trustworthy you would hand me the keys. Now let's say that I bring you back your car and I have torn it to pieces. The muffler is hanging off the bottom, the front quarter panel needs to be replaced, the back seat is torn and the motor is now making this funny ticking noise. You now have to go through the trouble of fixing everything that I messed up and some of it could be costly. The next time I ask to borrow your car what are you going to say? How about, NO?!?

In this analogy, I am the flesh and your car is your life. The flesh comes to you and asks you to borrow your life to go have some fun. It promises not to mess it up too much but then it does. It causes pain and sadness in relationship and at work. Some of it can be fixed but some if it is like that ticking sound that the motor is making. How am I going to fix that? Will I need a major overhaul or will I need to replace the engine? But the sad part is that the flesh is a good friend and even a better salesman. He will come again and say can I please borrow your body. Were gonna have so much fun and I promise this time I will bring it back in one piece. Even if I do put a little scratch on it the fun we will have will far outweigh the damage. And so we continue to give in until we learn to say no to the flesh. We say no by believing that Christ has something far better planned for our future than that car ride. We trust that the car ride is nothing more than a mud pie in the slums and he is offering a holiday at sea. We have faith that He has our best interest at heart and a plan for everything that we are going through.

So as I continued to progress in learning how to listen to the Spirit I wondered when God would show me what my favorite color was. I kept my mind open for anything that he had planned for me and waited patiently till the moment finally came. And believe me it was another home run completely out of the ballpark! It was fall of 2007 and the leaves that year were incredibly vibrant. I wasn't sure if they were always that bright or if they just seemed so vivid to me that year since color was starting to return into my life. I was progressing through my feelings chart and marking different feelings as God revealed to me what they felt like. Each day I was starting to feel a little more human.

I was headed to work for a meeting one morning and was driving slowly in a line of cars down Crabapple Road. The song playing on my radio was by Steve Fee and really struck a chord with my heart as it talked about broken people learning to be free and being able to lift their chains high as they celebrated their freedom from bondage. It really made me want to find my favorite color so I could free the little boy locked inside the walls of the castle.

Broken people call His name
Helpless children praise the King
Nothing brings Him greater fame
When broken people call His name

Lift high, your chains undone
All rise, exalt the Son
Jesus Christ, the Holy One
We lift our eyes to You

As the song played I noticed a tree on the side of the road up ahead. It was a Bradford Pear tree which turns a deep shade of blood red in the fall. As the wind blew and the leaves fell from the tree it appeared as if giant drops of beautiful healing crimson blood were falling to the ground. Tears began to fill my eyes as I heard the line from the song play. "Lift high your chains undone!!! All rise, exalt the Son." I was crying so hard that I had to pull the car over. I pulled my car over near the tree, got out of my car, and in my suit and tie sat down on the ground under the tree to let the blood of Christ wash over my soul. How do you script a moment like this?!? I would dare say that moments like this are only available from the Almighty and can only be experienced when we give up our rights to what we want and what we think we deserve and let Him give us what He has had planned for us all along.

Oh, by the way... this amazing moment is not yet over. As I sat under the tree crying, gathering a few leaves from the tree to keep in my journal and experiencing healing, I looked across the street and saw a maple tree. Again the wind picked up and blew the tree into a frenzy, but the leaves did not fall from this tree. This tree appeared to be the center of a raging passionate fire as the leaves flew upward and into the sky towards the heavens! And again the Holy Spirit came to speak to me the first few lines of a poem. It was time to come out of the gray and have a favorite color to call my own.

Out of the Gray

The young man is now yearning
To find a color of his own
To figure out what he feels inside
And let God show him his new tone

He digs deep into his soul
And gives God permission to let him feel
What has been buried in the dark from the past
Another layer of the onion to peel

It is not pretty, it doesn't feel good
But he knows it is somewhere he must go
Deep into his wounded heart
And give God a chance to sew

As he drives down the road and all is gray
God speaks through vision and song
I have wonderful plans for you my son
I know you have been waiting so long

You have suffered much pain while here on this earth
I know you have questions for me
Why must one suffer so
The fairness is hard to see

Look in front of you son
Look up and you will see
The Fire and Passion I hold inside
And the blood that I shed on Calvary

The young man looks up with hope in his eyes
He sees a tree burning as if on fire
Another tree is filled with blood
The sight fills him with desire

The trees are so deeply red
As they shine so vivid and so bright
At this moment they cannot compare
To any other colors in sight

I bled for you, my child and my son
My goal was to show all my love
I wanted to pull you close to my chest
And send you my grace on the wings of a dove

You are my fire, you are my passion
My blood many will see
Through your tears and your pain
My story of hope will ring free

Share your color with as many as you can
For with it my blood will flow
Focus solely on my love
And the fire and passion will grow

You are my fire, you are my passion
I bled for you, you bled for me
Be my fire, be my passion

bc

I showed up late for my meeting that morning and really was trying to hold it together emotionally. It can be hard for anyone not on a journey like this to understand what you are going through. I had tried to share what I was going through with a couple of people and was met with wide eyes, blank stares and judgmental eyes. I came to notice that I couldn't share what I was experiencing with most people because most people have not had these types of experiences. Most people have not had them because they have not asked for them. Until we want revelation we will not ask for it. When we are not wanting it and asking for it our heart is not prepared for it and we would not even be able to see it if God did give it to us. Do you think I would have noticed the trees and the song had my heart not been prepared for it?

I remember hearing someone tell a story of incredible faith where they needed milk for their child and someone showed up at the door saying that God told them to bring milk to their door. Or an entire orphanage filled with children sitting down to pray for dinner and no food was in the kitchen and a knock at the door reveals a broken down refrigerated truck looking to give away the food before it spoils. Upon hearing these stories I remember asking God to give me an experience like that. The problem was that I had a lot of money and bought anything I wanted whenever I wanted it. I was relying on me for my provision and did not know how to rely on God. I guess that's why scripture says that it is easier for a camel to go through the eye of a needle than it is for a rich man to find God.

As I went through the process of brokenness and reached the last $5 in the bank account I was distraught, depressed and had no idea what to do. When I woke up that morning I knew that I needed diapers for my handicapped daughter and food for dinner that night. I was tired of fretting, worrying and feeling like a total failure so I knelt down and asked God to provide what I needed for that day. As soon as I was done praying I received a call from someone in my small group who asked if I knew anyone who could put up some crown molding in their living and dining room. They did not know that I had grown up as a carpenter. They did not know that I had all of the tools necessary including laser levels and 5 nail guns in the basement. At this point the market was so bad I had not considered pulling out all my tools and going back to manual labor. In the past my pride would not have allowed me to stoop back down into manual labor. My identity would have said that I am a business man. What if someone sees me? I told them I would be over to look at it right away, hung up the phone and began to cry. I had asked for faith building experiences and I had gotten it! I had just experienced the raw faith it takes to depend on God for my daily bread.

When you begin this journey, God will send the right people at the right time to walk with you. I am so thankful for my good friend Michele. I met her at the same time that I started my 10 month program and she understood what it was like to grow up the way I did. She would take me to lunch and be a sounding board for the things that I was going through that I didn't quite understand. Most importantly, she showed me the positive love and affirmation that Christ was trying to show me. When looking for people to walk with as you grow, make sure they possess these very important traits and that they support you in love and guide you in love. Do not allow the pressure of adamancy to come back into your life. God cannot be free to work when adamancy and our egos are present.

I shared my second poem with my friend Michele and we laughed and cried together. The next morning as she left her neighborhood a beautiful red maple caught her eye as it was... you guessed it... coming out of the gray fog. She was thoughtful enough to stop and snap this picture which was the perfect metaphor for what I had felt just days before. We affectionately call this picture, Out of the Gray.

You are my fire, you are my passion. That is a piece of the identity that God gave to me. I didn't have to create it because it was in me since before I was born. Do you believe that you too can have a faith building God experience like this? Have you asked God for it? Are you willing to lose everything you think you are so that He can give you infinitely more? I hope you are. I believe in you. More importantly, He believes in you.

Chapter 29
Revelation
Finding Forgiveness

Forgiveness, now that's a big word to swallow. So how do you forgive the unthinkable? What is it like to forgive? Does it mean I have to forget what they did to me? Does it mean I have to start having dinner with them every night and rebuild the relationship?

All good questions but I think a good place to start is to create two categories. First, who do I need to forgive and second, what have I done that I would like forgiveness for? Once we start to make changes in our life it really is easy to begin thinking about the pain that we caused others and run to them asking for forgiveness. It really is part of the natural growing process. The harder of the two is to let go of something that someone did to me especially if they have yet to apologize for it. We think we just might consider it if they would deliver an apology that was good enough or genuine in nature.

Because it is the harder of the two and the foundation for all future growth, let's focus on the first category. Start by making a list of the people that have contributed something into your life that has caused you pain, sadness, or discomfort and now you hold them in any sort of disregard. At this point it doesn't really matter how small we believe the infraction is. Our goal is to get it all out of our head and onto paper so that God can let us know where He would like to begin. I hope you're starting to notice a pattern here. Not how I would like to proceed. How God leads me to proceed. The more you get what you want to do out of the way the sooner you will start to hear the peaceful genuine at rest leading of the Holy Spirit.

The usual laundry list can be easy, as it will be filled with relationships both present and past, parents, children, business partners, co-workers, pastors, friends, church members, teachers, etc. Add everyone to the list that you can think of that you believe owes you an apology or reparations for what they did that affected your life. At this point we aren't going to do anything other than make the list. It is not time to forgive yet. If you rush into forgiveness without going deep you can get incomplete forgiveness. I actually had 3 forgiveness sessions for my Father till I went deep enough to remove all of the poison that kept the wound from healing.

The main idea behind forgiveness is to allow a wound that was caused by someone else to be able to heal. Forgiveness is not really for the person you are forgiving as much as it is for you. It has been said that un-forgiveness is the poison that I will drink in the hopes that you will die. Complete forgiveness may take time so that you can make sure that all of the barbs and thorns inside the wound are removed before the wound is closed up. If you close up the wound with a thorn still inside the wound will still fester and hurt and there is a great likelihood that the wound will eventually reopen.

So what is up with the whole idea of forgive and forget? This idea generally comes from the fact that God says that He not only forgives our sins but that He also will forget them. God has the capacity to accomplish this because... well, because He's God. He is able to do both at the same time. Nothing in scripture exists that tells us that we will be able to forget an event in our life. Now, our failing memory as we age or a repressed event are the exceptions to this idea.

Let's talk a little bit about those repressed memories. There are events that will take place such as mine that are so traumatic that our mind will bury the memories deep down inside in an attempt to protect us from the reality that occurred and then even try to create an alternate reality for us to hold on to that is much more palatable than what actually happened.

If this is the case then you may have an inkling feeling that something is buried deep down inside and you need to ask God a few questions. Is it time for the buried memory to be brought to light and will you, God, hold my heart gently in your hands while this event surfaces? I hold a special place in my heart for anyone that makes the decision to bring up this type of event. It will be a painful process to open a wound that has been previously shut but you will be rewarded with an experience of peace and healing beyond what you can imagine. It is important not to attempt to travel this part of the path alone. You must allow God and a close group of friends walk with you down this path of bringing what has been dark for so long into the light. Maybe you too will have your own 'Out of the Gray' moment in your life.

It is more important than ever at this point to remember not to manufacture events from the past. It will be very easy to start to feed off of the sympathy that many will feel as moments from the past surface and begin to manufacture and embellish on what took place. If God does say that it is your time, he will do the work in bringing what is dark into the light. All you have to do put on your seatbelt, lock yourself in for a bumpy ride, and surrender your feelings and the entire process and outcome to a more than capable God. Remember that we must believe that He is finishing the work that He started in us and that He is faithful in His promises even when it looks like there is no end in sight. It may take several months to a year to uncover so you will need to remember to stay focused and intent on the process.

A major awareness at this point will be to watch that you do not adopt the victim mentality. This type of thinking can keep us locked for many years in a helpless state where we blame everything on our terrible situation. I'm sure you can think of someone right now that is living the victim role and you can see the damage that it has done to their life. The goal in uncovering what is buried is not to assume the role of victim but to remove all poison from the wound so that it has the ability to heal. The victim never stops carrying the pain of an event and uses the event as their identity. This identity can either be cast in a positively charged light such as "I am a tough son of a bitch because of what happened to me and everyone can kiss my ass", or it can be negatively charged in an attitude of "Woe is me and the world is coming to an end". Either way, the idea is to make sure that your goal is to get past the event when the time is right and not to linger longer than necessary in this stage.

Now whether your event is buried and you uncover it or on the surface and you can clearly define it, the next few steps will be the same. Step 1 will be to feel the pain and anger of what happened to you for as long as necessary. Many people will come along and tell you that anger is not part of this process and want you to move straight to forgiveness. If all of the anger is not removed from the wound you will close it up with the anger still inside.

One of my favorite books that covers forgiveness is called "The Shack" by William Young. In this book the author tells of a garden that looks very beautiful and represents the life of a young man with pain at his very core that he does not know how to forgive. Upon seeing his garden a day later the entire beautiful centerpiece of the garden has been ripped out and the Holy Spirit was digging deep into the center of it. The man asked him why He had removed all of the beautiful flowers that were covering the center of the garden. The Holy Spirit told him that everything beautiful that had been planted was covering up something that would not allow anything in the rest of the garden to grow to its full potential. What was already pretty had to be removed so that God could dig deeper to remove what was inhibiting much needed growth and then plant new seed in the ground.

Such may be the case in our lives. We may have covered an event that we are very angry about with a lovely array of flowers. These flowers are our current identity as on the surface they show people what we want them to see, It may be time to remove those flowers and dig deep to feel the pain and sadness necessary for healing. Go ahead and feel the anger until God tells you it is time to stop feeling the anger. He will let you know when the time is right for you to move on to the next step. I felt the anger towards my father for almost an entire year. I once told my small group that I was so angry that if he walked in here right now I would rip his arms off and beat him with his own arms. Don't hold back or run from the feeling. Feel it for everything it is worth.

If the event happened as a child, try to feel the event as the child would have felt it. As adults we have the ability to rationalize what we see. When we rationalize for the person that did the event we lessen the impact of the feelings of the child. As an adult I know that my father was beaten as a child and I can offer him some compassion and understand why he was so angry. The child was not able to rationalize with this information and thus the feeling of the event should be felt as the child felt it at the time.

Let's take a look at another analogy. A young girl spends several days drawing the perfect birthday card for her father and is giddy about the moment that she will surprise him with it as he walks out the door for work. The morning of his birthday he wakes up late, gets into an argument with mom, the coffee pot breaks and does not make his coffee. Last week at work he was given a big project that he feels he is failing at and he wonders if he is going to lose his job. As he rushes down the stairs to run out the door the little girl is waiting, card in her hand and big smile on her face. At this point he may not even remember it is his birthday because of all of the events going on combined. As he hurriedly runs past her she tries to stop him and he yells at her to get out of the way. He is late for work and he doesn't have time for her right now.

Now let me ask you this? Is the little girl able to say, "It's ok daddy. I understand what you're going through and I will be here for you when you get home to help you ease the stress." She is not. What does she feel? Unimportant, uncared for, unworthy – She is crushed! The feelings quickly lead to beliefs. Daddy doesn't care about me. I am insignificant. I am unimportant. I don't matter. Maybe no one cares about me. Maybe I just need to take care of myself. Her beliefs then lead to how she will cope with the pain of the event. I'm never doing that again. She will withdraw from giving gifts because she was hurt in the process of giving. And now she is 32 years old wondering why she can't trust who she is dating. Wondering why she can't rely on anyone else or believe that they could really love her enough to care for her. Because remember, her belief system tells her that she is not worthy. No event is too small. Pull out your journal and ask God to bring to your mind the events that cast false belief into your life.

Step 2 on the path to forgiveness must not be skipped over. Missing step 2 will be the difference between being ok with what is going on and having everyone around you standing 20 feet away wondering if you're going to blow and making sure they keep their distance. No matter how much you want to hold on to the rage step 2 adds surrender into the mix. Step 2 – Every night release the anger you are feeling to God and ask Him to share it with you. This step is sort of like the safety valve on a pressure cooker. Without it the pressure would build until the pot explodes. It also helps us to make sure that we feel the anger but that we don't let it consume us or become our identity. If people around you start to comment on how angry that you are than it is definitely time to release your anger to God. He can handle it and He will carry your burden with you and for you when you need it most.

Once you have felt the anger for all it is worth and the level of anger begins to subside than you are ready to move to step 3. Step 3 – Mourn the loss. Every infraction carries with it a debt to debtor relationship. The person who has hurt me has taken something from me and must therefore pay. You must identify what it is that has been taken from you and mourn the loss of it. In a relationship the debt may be love, time, money, emotion or any number of things. In my case I had to mourn the loss of a childhood. My parents could not give me another childhood so I have the choice of either holding this debt against them for the rest of their lives or of releasing the debt as paid in full. I do not choose to release the debt for their benefit. I choose to release it for me and my own peace. I also can choose to release it because the same was done for me. Christ gave me the gift of forgiveness for all I had done and now that I have received it I can choose to pass it on to others.

All of the same rules that applied to feeling the anger also apply to mourning. Mourn until God let's you know that it is time to move on to the next step, do not get stuck in mourning as a victim that needs to have a pity party every conversation of every day and do not draw your identity from it. Your anger or mourning is not who you are, it is just a stage in the forgiveness and healing process. So cry as much as you need to. If tears do not come, ask God to bring them to you. Tears have the power to cleanse and heal your inner soul. Shake free the words you heard as a child that told you not to cry. It's ok to allow your tears to come in and cleanse your heart. Give God permission and then give it to yourself.

Once you have completed all of the stages your heart and mind should be prepared to let go, forgive the debt that is owed and wipe the slate clean. Here is a recap of the steps to make sure that you have addressed each one and removed any of the poison left in the wound. Once we identify a debt that is owed we will:

1. Feel the anger, hurt, pain and sadness of the event
2. Release the anger and hurt every night
3. Mourn the loss
4. Forgive the debt as we surrender it to God

I found forgiveness for my father after reading the book I mentioned before called The Shack. In the months prior to reaching the final few chapters of The Shack I had spent 3 months feeling anger and another 3 months mourning the loss of my childhood. In the beginning of the book the main character named Mack receives a letter in the mailbox from God. The letter asked Mack to meet God in the shack where his daughter was killed. Can you imagine the feeling this man must have had? How dare God ask me to come back to that place of all places? The brilliant metaphor by the writer of course is that God is waiting for each of us at the source of our greatest pain. And in order for us to get past whatever this event is we must realize what and where our 'shack' is and go back there. In that moment we may have lost who we were created to be and put on a new identity. We may have picked up the identity that the event gave us. We are in a fallen world where people get shot, raped, beaten, killed, harassed, and violated in many ways and many times it seems for absolutely no reason. We may never know why and the question of why will keep us holding tightly to the event. God is waiting for you at the source of your greatest pain. If you knew it meant that your life would finally be at peace, would you go meet with him in that shack? Would you be willing to forgive the unforgivable?

Even before I reached the end of the book I knew what God was preparing me for. I knew he wanted me to forgive the man that had beaten a small fragile little boy to the point that he wanted to die. He wanted me to forgive a mother that did nothing to stop him. He wanted me to let go of the identity that I was a mean son of a bitch because of what they did to me and put on the identity of freedom! Freedom from the oppression that ruled my soul and freedom from the hatred that lived in my heart.

So I called a few friends and asked them for their help and support in forgiving my parents. We met in a small room and placed my imaginary parents in the chair across from me one at a time. They placed their hands on me and prayed for strength and courage as I recounted out loud every time that they hurt me and every event that allowed them to hold power over me. I released each of them from the debt that they owed me. As I left that room with my shirt soaked in tears I heard the voice of God singing in my mind "It is finished – the battle is over." That night I slept like a baby held in the arms of his true loving Father.

Please take this time to write in your journal who you need to forgive and what they owe you. It makes me smile as I think of the smile on your face and the peace in your heart as you walk out of your forgiveness session and into freedom. The freedom song ringing in your ears with chains broken and lifted high above your head. Perhaps you too will hear your own song from God's heart to your heart. It is finished – the battle is over.

Chapter 30
Revelation

The Most Important Forgiveness

In the previous chapter we discussed forgiveness of other people that have wronged you. What I have learned throughout this process is that there are two people that will end up taking the blame in practically any and every situation. These two people are thrown under the bus and dragged for not just months and years, but for lifetimes. They are the hardest two people to forgive and at the same time the most important. One of them you are looking at in the mirror and the other is the one who you believe is responsible for what you are looking at in the mirror – that's right, it's you and God.

Take a moment to think about the victim in any altercation. We may start by trying to blame the attacker or instigator of our event but ultimately the blame works its way back to us. I should have been stronger. I could have stood up for myself. I was too weak. If only I had gone a different way home this wouldn't have happened to me. And then it seems that we can't help but wallow in the randomness of the event which leads to the conclusion that God must be responsible for either allowing this to happen or causing this to happen. Either way, both my identity and my perception of God are altered because of the event.

My identity is altered because I may live for years with the thought process that I am to blame for being beaten. I may even begin to believe that I am bad and I deserve to be punished. This may lead to a life of failure because I don't believe that I deserve to be a success because I am bad. Once this belief sets in I may also go through life sabotaging every good thing that ever happens to me. I may find a good job or a stable relationship and then something inside me gets very uncomfortable so I burn it to the ground.

And don't forget how closely God is related to this as well. His identity to me has now changed. Instead of me believing that He has the best in mind for me, I now believe that He must hate me or that He must be so disappointed in me.

Well what if we threw an entirely new belief in to the mix here? What if I believed that He is my creator and knew everything that I was going to do before I did it? If He knew me before I was born than why would He now be disappointed when I did what He already knew that I was going to do. Remember that this all stems back to belief. What I believe about God and myself will control my life. If I believe I am a loser and a failure I will live that out in my life. If I believe that I am beautiful and a child loved by God my Father as He holds me gently in His arms, then that is how I will live my life. Think of how much easier it would be to forgive someone if I saw myself accordingly. Think of the arguments that would never take place if you felt that way. I no longer would have to fight for what I think I want. I no longer would have to fight for love, acceptance, worth and security because I would accept what was being freely offered and believe that I deserve it. Not because I earned it but simply because my father says that I am worth it.

Can you accept that? Can you accept that you do not have to do anything to receive that from Him? We spend all our lives following the world's standards for how we attain wealth and riches so it can be difficult to understand that someone would love me enough to give me this gift without me having to do anything to earn it. We may have even spent many years trying to earn it, trying to be good enough, trying to prove that we truly deserve it. But the kingdom He has created is not of this world.

Can you imagine the look on people's faces as Jesus gave The Sermon on the Mount? The meek shall inherit the earth? What is He talking about? Is He crazy? This guy doesn't know what He is talking about. The world believes that the strong will rule the earth.

This is another one of those beliefs from the past that we need to question. Every belief that originated from the world's point of view only allows us to see what is in the world. Paul speaks in Romans of what is seen in this world and what is unseen. How many times have you heard people say "Oh, well God just doesn't work that way anymore." Guess what. If that is your belief then that is what will be true for you. Since I began to allow God to reveal Himself to me in any way He chooses, I have seen and experienced things that are unseen in this world that would blow your mind over and over again. You might even tell me that I'm crazy and of course many of you would say, "Oh, well, God just doesn't work that way anymore." Well why not. Did He come tell you this or have you just not seen it. And have you not seen it because you do not believe that it is possible?

As you venture out from the world that most accept as the norm and begin to unplug from the rules and structure of religion and society there will be those that ridicule and try to bring you back to their reality. These people will not understand where you are going and why because they are not on the narrow path. I am sorry to say but our friends who have not chosen to walk the narrow path will not be able to see what is unseen. But we cannot be discouraged. We must remember why we started this journey and hold on tightly to God and the people that are on the path with us.

This leads us back to our discussion on the two most

important people to forgive. We can be so terribly difficult on ourselves. It may be time to ask yourself if you are ready to let you and God come down off of the cross. Are you ready to experience the life that He is offering? Go through the steps for forgiveness listed in the previous chapter and apply them one at a time for you and for God.

Plan a forgiveness session where you list everything that you are holding against God. In my session I blamed him for my horrible childhood, my daughter's illness, the loss of my business and home and much more. Do you really think he can't handle it or doesn't already know? He wants to heal every hurt that we have experienced in this broken world. If you don't believe that then you are right in your mind and will live your life accordingly. If you do believe it, the way you are able to live will be drastically different.

Plan a forgiveness session where you list everything that you hold against yourself and let it all go. I have even attended sessions where all of these events are written on paper, physically nailed to a cross, and then each piece of paper is burned to ashes symbolizing that they are gone forever. I remember being so scared of who I would be if I forgave myself that I didn't want to go through with it. But then a friend on the path with me came to me with a bucket of water and he washed my feet. As the water ran over my feet all I could feel was the hands of my Savior washing away all that I had held against myself and our Father. Probably one of the most healing moments I can ever remember in my entire life. But it wasn't the last. The work of God is ongoing and always in process. It only stops when we stop and decide that we have arrived.

Another great analogy on forgiveness that I want to share with you also comes from The Shack. Once forgiveness takes place the deceiver will come in and try to steal that forgiveness from you. Religious people who think they know everything will try to tell you what forgiveness is and what you have to do to know that you have forgiven. I remember someone telling me that I had to go have dinner with my dad once a week to prove that I had forgiven him. I think the important thing here is not to let anyone try to define what forgiveness looks like in your situation. Forgiveness is more about removing the wedge between you and God than it is about removing it from between you and the other person. Once that wedge is removed and you have released control of the situation, the Holy Spirit will organically orchestrate whatever it is that is supposed to happen when it is supposed to happen. So many times when I tried to orchestrate healing events that I was goaded into by 'friends', I messed things up badly.

It is impractical to think that any of us would have to go to a weekly dinner or on a vacation with someone who had abused us in the past. In some cases God may ask you to do something absolutely extreme like this. The important thing to remember here is that God is only asking for us to get out of the way and let Him do the work that we cannot do.

Once you have had your forgiveness session the deceiver will visit very soon and try to convince you that you are still angry. He will remind you what that person did and try to convince you that this person still owes you a debt. What we have to do is remind ourselves that the there is no debt. I forgave that debt. I may have to remind myself 50 times that week that I forgave that man for what he did. In week 2 maybe I only have to remind myself 20 times. In month 2 I may only have to remind myself 10 times the whole month until finally the deceiver loses the power he had over me when the event fades away because I know that the debt has been paid and he owes me absolutely nothing.

Pull out your journal and ask God to reveal to you what you are holding against Him that He would like you to let go of. Ask Him to reveal to you what you are holding against yourself. We are our own worst critic. You may be hanging on a cross that you believe God and religion has nailed you to. Close your eyes as you journal and look into your own hands. You may reveal the hammer that you have used to nail yourself to the cross. Is it time to forgive yourself? No matter how bad it is, God has forgiven you and the only way he can step in to show you who you truly are is if you finally forgive yourself. It is time to finally let it go.

Chapter 31
Revelation and Redemption

And the Seed Becomes a Rose

As you look at the beauty of a rose have you ever stopped to think about how that rose made it to where it is in life? It wasn't always so glamorous nor was it born that way. Unfortunately, it had to endure its growing pains to reach the moment where it stands tall in the sun and broadcasts its glorious beauty in every direction. Not only that, but what is it that the rose did in its own power to reach this penultimate moment. The only thing it did was receive. It allowed the one who planted it to water the ground, fertilize the soil, plant and replant as needed, and till the earth around it to cultivate new growth.

As I neared the end of my 10 month class a specific phrase began to ring in my mind over and over. 'A seed was planted long ago, planted deep in the ground by the One who loves me so.' I knew right away that this was the line of another amazing gift from the One I now completely accepted and knew as my Father. I had been learning to trust again and slowly but surely dismantling the walls of my castle. This process exhibited many ups and downs as the child was released into the world. Many times I exhibited childish tendencies and pitched temper tantrums accompanied by pouting and the silent treatment.

What I came to find out in therapy sessions was that when an adult begins to feel again after being locked up since childhood, that they will act the usual emotion of that age. This includes the actions that come with being 8 years old! Can you imagine an adult acting emotionally like an 8 year old? Well, maybe some of you can imagine that easier than others. Or at least we can think of 'a friend' that is like that. Wink Wink. With my emotions being that of an 8 year old just being released to feel again, I pressed forward with the goal of learning and understanding each emotion I was feeling.

Understanding my emotional age allowed me to be able to forgive myself each time I acted out and also caused me to be open for growth as my emotional age developed. As a young Christian I stumbled and made many mistakes. In fact, most of what I have learned and shared in the pages of this book about freedom from adamancy and self involvement, I learned from my failures and mistakes. It is hurtful to think of the people around me who were wounded along my path to brokenness and recovery. As I neared the end of my 10 month program I sought out many of those people and asked for their forgiveness for the things that they experienced due to my impetuous nature.

Now that I had found out how to let go of the things that I was holding on to I felt more relaxed. No longer did every day feel like a fight to keep my head screwed on straight. As I sit here thinking about all of the feelings I have now learned to feel I am thankful for each person that God brought into my life to walk with me on the narrow path. I am thankful that every step of the way God has been there with me as He helped me learn to hear His voice. Some of you may be thinking that you to would like to walk down this path. Hopefully you have already headed in that direction.

Remember that your first step is to activate the promise that He so graciously offered to us. Ask and you will receive, seek and you will find, knock and the door will be opened. He wants you to know what is on the other side of that door, but you have to be the one that knocks. He will not force anything on you. This is also the confusing part of the journey where many people end up quitting. I have had people tell me that they asked God to come into their life to help them and then everything started going wrong. This is usually when we cry out and say, "Hold on a minute God, I asked for you to help me and now everything is going to hell in a hand basket." But this is where we will be tempted to quit. Once we activate the promise, once we let God know that we have tried to be king of our lives and failed, once we ask Him to show us who He is, once we ask Him to be king in our lives, the conflict in our lives will be more evident. The good news is that happiness will also come because it is the counterpart to sadness.

The best realization that I have ever had about happiness was that I did not know what it really felt like because I did not let myself feel sadness. If I choose to turn off the feeling of sadness, happiness has to go right along with it. We cannot have the pleasure without the pain. We will not experience the beauty without walking through the ugliness. This principle is scattered all throughout nature. If you have ever experienced the incredible pain of childbirth followed by the beauty of holding a newborn baby you know the truth of this principle.

This point was shown to me in true vivid color one day as I rode my bike down a trail in the woods. It was late February and everything in the forest was dead and waiting for the spring to arrive. As I rounded a corner on the trail I saw a giant hornet coming straight at me. I tried to duck down to the get under it but it hit me stinger first right in the shoulder! The instant pain was excruciating and almost mind numbing as I reached up with one hand to try to pull the giant hornet out from being embedded in my left shoulder. Of course I then realize that I am moving down the trail at about 15 to 20 miles per hour in a curve with only one hand on the handlebars. With that one hand I applied the brake which happened to be the front brake. Any of you who ride bikes know what happened next. That's right, head over heels! It really was a spectacular wreck. I flipped several times and as I came to a stop I jumped to my feet quickly in an attempt to walk/jog off the pain.

Normally, at this point I would have cussed up a storm and screamed at the universe for sending a random hornet into my life to mess up my day. It used to seem like almost every day was a random hornet day. And I would go through each of those days cursing as each one reared its ugly head. But now I have learned how to feel the pain and look for its counterpoint. If there is pain, somewhere nearby is beauty. And If I am going to submit to the pain I don't want to be the one that decides to quit just before the beauty shows up. And so at the end of my spectacular flip over the handlebars and into the woods, I sat down in the forest amongst the trees and reached up and pulled the hornet from my shoulder. I closed my eyes and I breathed in the pain for everything it was worth and opened my eyes to see something amazing! A single, solitary red flower, all alone growing in the midst of a lifeless forest! As I stared at its beauty I realized what this flower meant to me. The flower was me growing out of the death and the gray fog that had surrounded me my whole life. This flower gave me hope to believe that I would be healed and feel whole again. I instantly saw myself as a flower in a field growing taller and taller but this time not surrounded by death – surrounded by other flowers with endless beauty.

Why do I tell you this story? It really is because every day of my life is still a random hornet day. There are things that still go wrong and cause me pain. There are still things that happen that I would like to run from. But now I embrace each of them because I believe that each event is intended to teach me something new about God and about myself. I believe that each event has beauty hidden somewhere in its folds. Why do you think we call them 'growing pains'? When we ask God for that beauty, for that change, we must be prepared to walk all the way through whatever is necessary to reach it. Don't be the one that stops right before you get to see the beauty. If it were not for the hornet, I would never have seen my red flower growing out of nothing. I would have missed this beautiful picture of God's amazing redemption and the opportunity to encourage others with such an amazing story of hope.

We started this chapter by talking about a seed and a rose. The line given to me by God continued to ring over and over. "A seed was planted long ago. Planted deep in the ground by the One who loves me so." I began to think about the seed and even though I was feeling like the rose I was realizing what a seed had to go through to become a rose. First of all, the seed doesn't know anything other than being a seed. It doesn't even know that it has the capacity to be something so beautiful. It only knows life as a seed. That's why trust is so important. I'm sure you have noticed in this book what I like to call faith building experiences. As you will recall, I started out not believing in God. How did that change? It changed when I got out of the way and gave Him permission to remove everything that I thought I was no matter how painful it would be, and replace it with who He created me to be.

The next thing we can notice about the seed was that it has to go into the cold dark ground and wait for a long period of time before it can germinate and begin to grow. And before it can germinate, it has to die. That's right, it has to die to who it thinks it is as a seed so that it can become something that it cannot even imagine – a beautiful red rose.

The poem took shape as I graduated from my 10 month class and I shared it with the people who had walked with me as I had been picked apart, dismantled, crushed, broken, put back together and beautifully reborn. I share it now with you in hopes that you too will see that even if you are the seed, you too have the potential, if you are willing... to become the rose.

The Seed

A seed was planted long ago
Planted deep in the ground
By the One who loves me so

The process all began
One crisp, cool autumn day
The wind was blowing gently
And the leaves were going their own way

A young seed sat and wondered
Trapped deep inside his self centered mind
Could he do anything more in himself
To become more loving and kind

He's resigned to the fact that there is nothing more
He's gone as deep as he can go
Everyone has their demons and pain
Locked up safe in the dungeons below

Never to let them out
Don't let anyone see you sweat or cry
My demons tell me who I am
They never give me the chance to fly

But a seed was planted long ago
Planted deep in the ground
By the One who loves me so

He prepared the soil so gentle and kind
And placed the seed deep in the ground
His love child growing ever so slowly
But feeling he will never be found

The seed did not know the plan of the master
Nor did he know the potential of what he would become
He simply sat every day in the dark
Growing colder, full of fear, and more numb

The seed sat through autumn and winter
And began to feel the pains that come with change
Cold and frozen in ice so strong
Would it ever again see the sun on the range

He remembered being a seed in the past
He remembered it wasn't so bad
Lost above ground with everyone else
But at least warm and dry and with illusions of being glad

But a seed was planted long ago
Planted deep in the ground
By the One who loves me so

Why did He put me down here in the ground
In places so dark and so low
Didn't He say he loved me so much
His actions surely don't show

The pressure of the ground is crushing me inside
Soon, I know that I will break
Into angry little pieces never to be fixed
The pain may be more than I can take

I surrender to the pain and give in to my death
It seems the only path I have not tried
All my quick fixes and failures
Have done nothing but affect my pride

What's this I feel? It's a warmth from above
The ground is beginning to thaw
The spring is here and new life can begin
Because of surrender and death of the law

A seed was planted long ago
Planted deep in the ground
By the One who loves me so

The Son's love is glowing down
And all I can feel is the heat
Something is happening, I cannot tell what
But it's something amazing and sweet

This warmth is intoxicating
As it holds me tightly in its embrace
I'm still in the dark and scared to death
My control I exchange gladly for His grace

My death places all my pain behind me
As I feel something new beginning to emerge
I've never felt this way before
As new green growth begins to surge

First a crack and then a push
And now I see some light
The tears are streaming down my face
As I look back on my journey and my plight

The One I love is smiling down
And showering me with His love
He collects my tears and shelters me
With His wings so soft like a dove

A seed was planted long ago

Planted deep in the ground
By the One who loves me so

Daily He waters me
And warms me in the Son
With this new life I'm growing so fast
It's so much easier than the old one

Father says it's time to see
Why we've worked so hard
Why we had to go through it all
And be buried so long in the yard

I feel tall, clean, and glorified
As I dance slowly in the Son
Father casts my gaze to the end of my branch
I'm in awe of what has been done

For the seed has become a beautiful red rose
With brilliance that cannot compare
The passion and fire burns bright from the rose
With compassion, love, and deep care

How could the seed have ever known
What was at the end of the show
All it took was surrender and trust
In the One who loves him so

But a seed was planted long ago
Planted deep in the ground
By the One who loves me so

And the Seed with the Son's love becomes a Rose

bc

233

What if the seed didn't allow itself to be put into the ground? What if it had refused and decided that it was just easier to keep being a seed? I hope that somehow out of my story that you can see that it doesn't matter what your story is, you too can be the rose. Hopefully you can use the tools that I found along my journey to find your way past every excuse that makes you believe that the rose just isn't possible for you. I have repeatedly told you that I believed in you throughout this book but I know that isn't going to be enough. At some point you have to believe in you. Hopefully you can now begin to believe that no matter what you did or what was done to you, God is good and He wants you to ask Him to put you into the ground so that you can start the process of becoming the rose.

After graduation I joked with my classmates that we now have diplomas and that we are now completely fixed and don't need any more therapy. We all laughed together because we now understand that we will never be done growing and learning. Because there is always room for growth on the path to peace and once you know everything – you can't learn anything.

I love the story in the Bible where God is walking with Enoch every evening and one night in particular, Enoch is so close to God, that the two of them walk all the way home right into heaven. I guess that means that until I am walking with God and He and I walk into heaven together... I have further to walk on the path and deeper to go with my God.

Is today the day that you will allow God to finish the work that He has begun in you? Is today the day that you submit to being the seed? I hope so. If you make that decision I can promise you that the payoff is greater than anything that you can even imagine. Commit today to let go of everything that you are holding onto so tightly. Find a friend to help you walk the path. Let the love of God wash over you and accept that you are lovable and that you don't have to work for it. And remember that the seed, with the Son's love... becomes a rose.

www.ingramcontent.com/pod-product-compliance
Lightning Source LLC
Chambersburg PA
CBHW060046100426
42742CB00014B/2715